METALWORK
jewelry

35 step-by-step projects inspired by steampunk

LINDA PETERSON

CICO BOOKS

LONDON NEW YORK

THIS BOOK IS DEDICATED TO MY DAD, WHO IS MY ROCK AND
PILLAR OF STRENGTH... YOU ARE ME AND I AM YOUR MINI-ME!

This edition published in 2018 by CICO Books
An imprint of Ryland Peters & Small Ltd
20–21 Jockey's Fields, London WC1R 4BW
341 E 116th St, New York, NY10029
www.rylandpeters.com

10 9 8 7 6 5 4 3 2 1

First published in 2011 by CICO Books

A CIP catalog record for this book is available from the Library of
Congress and the British Library.

ISBN: 978-1-78249-653-3

Printed in China

Editor: Marie Clayton
Designer: Christine Wood
Design concept: Jerry Goldie
Step-by-step photography: Geoff Dann
Style photography: Stuart West
Styling and art direction: Luis Peral-Aranda

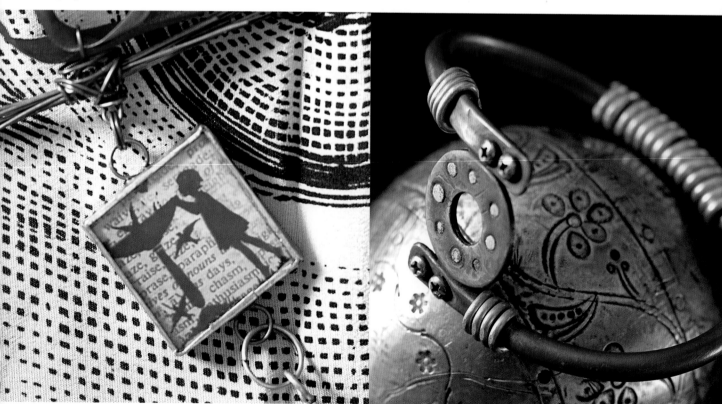

Contents

Introduction

When I was growing up, I was always hearing "One man's trash is another's treasure." My Mom and Grandma kept everything, from newspaper clippings and bottle caps to buttons and fabric scraps from a favorite shirt. My Grandma even kept an old Kewpie doll that was tattered, just because my baby cousin Julie's dirty fingerprints were on its face. I suppose to some people these things may have appeared to be nothing more than trash, but to Mom and Grandma they were priceless treasures, bringing back happy memories each time they looked at seemingly worthless objects.

I am confident that this explains why I find it impossible to throw anything away. Maybe, just maybe, it's the reason why my studio is filled to the brim with what I like to describe as hidden treasures—trinkets offer a view into my past. And beside the sentimental feelings from broken bits and pieces I've saved from family treasures, there also lies within me the "thrill of the hunt"—the search for unique, found objects: obscure things you would otherwise cast aside. Things such an old washer laying on a sidewalk, painted with a patina that only Mother Nature could provide; or perhaps a small brass bolt showing signs of gentle distress that I found on a bridge in Paris, France; or the dingy old typewriter, keys missing and tossed in the corner of a charity shop—otherwise useless, but calling out to me to take it home and resurrect it to a state of worth. It's a never-ending quest and when these objects find their way into my art, they are given a new outlook on life. As I look at each piece, my mind goes back to the hunt, the journey, and I relive the creative process. It is my happy place.

Designing for this book took me back to that happy place. It gave me permission to explore and create outside the typical square box, with no rules, limits, or guidelines. The designs reflect a variety of styles from "hardware chic" to a style that has been given the name "steampunk." The "hardware chic" designs in this book lend themselves to materials found at your local hardware store. Copper tubing, tiny nuts and bolts, and all kinds of electrical wire work together to create bold, chunky, and more contemporary-style "clunky"

jewelry. The "steampunk"-styled designs encompass a unique collection of materials that combine vintage with modern elements, fantasy with reality. Steampunk is reminiscent of an era powered by steam engines, so in this style you'll find lots of designs featuring gears and found objects combined with strips of fabrics and recycled denim. Soft and delicate meets chunky and bold.

If you are new to jewelry designing, don't let a lack of experience intimidate you. Familiarize yourself with the techniques section of the book, which will give you all the necessary skills to complete the projects. The very first project in the book combines elements often found in the scrapbooking section of your local arts and crafts store and uses basic jewelry-making techniques as a way to get you familiar working with the tools and assembling jewelry with jump rings. It's a "jump-start" project, if you will. As you progress through the first chapter you will even become acquainted with using materials that you might have otherwise have tossed aside, such as soda cans and soda tabs. In the next chapter, Wireworking and Found Objects, you'll take these skills further and work with all sorts of wire to create vintage-looking designs. Combine these with a variety of interesting textures and found objects to create one-of-a-kind designs. Finally, in the last chapter, you will advance to basic metalworking techniques such as soldering, working with copper tubing, forming metals, and more. These are all the stepping-stones you will need to create a wide variety of designs.

As you become familiar with the materials and build up confidence in your skills, challenge yourself to mix and match techniques to create your own designs. I guarantee it will open your eyes to a whole new world of seeing objects and giving them a new lease on life. And to illustrate this, a little story: after photographing the pictures for this book my editor, Marie, and I spent a couple of days in Paris. As I walked toward the Eiffel Tower, my eyes were affixed on the ground—yes, you guessed it… looking for stuff! However, I was not the only one. I looked over to find Marie, crouching down, digging a vintage bottle cap out of the ground with one of her car keys. And yes, I took her picture!

Enjoy your journey…

Linda

CHAPTER 1
Tools, Materials, & Techniques

Having the correct tools for the job will make your jewelry making a more pleasant experience—and much easier. With that said, there are loads of jewelry tools available and this section by no means covers them all. I've chosen those that I really feel will give the most for your money. This section also covers the techniques that will be used over again—a few additional one-off techniques are given in the relevant project.

Tools

It's not necessary to rush out and purchase lots of tools to begin with, but you will need a few tried-and-tested basics, which I have included in this section. Many tools can be found in local hardware stores, although some—such as dapping blocks and metal stamps—will only be found at specialty jewelry-making or lapidary stores. There are also many sources on the Internet.

PLIERS AND WIRE CUTTERS

Bail-making pliers
Used to create loops and rings in wire, or when creating decorative coils. These are also handy pliers to bend filigree findings to create custom bails.

Flat-nose pliers
The jaws of these have squared edges, so they are useful for sharp 90° angles. They are also handy to keep the coils flat and can be used to straighten bent wire. Choose a pair that has no teeth.

Concave bending pliers
Allows you to easily bend wire when forming it into rounded shapes to create loops for wire wrapping or bail making.

Basic jewelry pliers
Can be used when creating decorative coils. These generally have teeth that allow you to grip and pull wire tight, so be careful as the teeth may leave marks on the metal.

Round-nose pliers
Used to create loops and rings in wire, or when creating decorative coils. They are tapered so that you can make a variety of different-sized loops.

Standard wire cutters
These are useful for creating wire bails, making jump rings, and snipping off excess amounts of wire. They usually cut the wire end in a point.

SHAPING TOOLS

Dapping (or doming) block

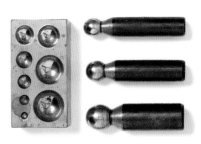

A block with different-sized concave domes, used with matching punches (a tool that has a steel shaft with a round ball at the end). To shape metal and form domed shapes, place the appropriate punch in the cavity and tap with a hammer. Cavities range from deep—such as those found in a steel block—to slight, as found in the wooden versions.

Ring mandrel

Used for sizing and creating rings. A bracelet mandrel is similar, yet much larger, and is used in a similar way for making and sizing bracelets.

CUTTING TOOLS

Hole punches

To create small holes in metals. There are several different types available, from those that are specifically made to punch through thicker metal to those that are general purpose. I have a selection of both.

Pipe cutter

Contains a cutting blade in the jaws so that you can grip and twist to slice sections from metal pipe.

Disk cutter

A metal block with circular holes and matching cylinder punches, to cut precise disks from soft metal sheet. Place the sheet in the slot in the side of the block and use a hammer to punch the cylinder through so that the disk drops out below.

Jeweler's saw

Similar to a small hacksaw, used to cut shapes from sheet metal.

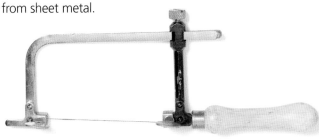

Scissors

Handy for trimming resin, and cutting lightweight sheet materials. I particularly like this brand, because they are durable and tough enough to cut softer metals such as thin aluminum and copper.

Cut Lube

A lubricant used to reduce friction and extend the life of a saw blade. Very useful and highly recommended.

HAMMERS

Ball-pein hammer
A heavyweight hammer; use the flat end to flatten metal and the ball end to texture.

Texturing hammer
Each head on this has a different face pattern, so when you hammer metal you can create a textured design. These come in a variety of different designs and are relatively inexpensive.

Nylon hammer
A double-ended hammer with one nylon head to avoid damaging more delicate components. The opposite head is metal to flatten thinner metals and wires. This is a handy hammer to have, since it has different ends on one hammer.

Chasing hammer
Used to hammer components flat, while the ball at the end can be used to create nice hammered texture effects in metal.

Bench block
This provides a firm, flat base for hammering. The rubber base serves as a cushion to absorb the force of the hammer and protects your work surface. You can flip this particular style of bench block over and use the rubberized side to polish; the rubber grips your pieces and prevents them from sliding around as you polish, making it a dual-purpose tool.

MARKING AND TEXTURING TOOLS

Rubber stamps
For adding design and pattern to components.

Ink pad
Used with the rubber stamps. The pigment-based ink is used to provide a resist when etching metals and can also be used to age and distress elements.

Letter punches
For stamping letters or words. These can be found in your local hardware store—they are used for stamping your name into your tools as a means of identification. Different type styles are also available at jewelry supply stores online.

Stylus, punch, and nail set
Wooden stylus for embossing metals, center punch to create an indentation so that the bit doesn't slip when starting to drill a hole, and a nail set used to create texture or make tiny circles when tapped into metal.

Rub 'N' Buff®
A rub-on wax finish that can be used to change the color of findings and to add highlighting to textured areas.

Alcohol inks (not shown)
Alcohol-based inks are useful for adding color. They dry quickly and are transparent.

POWER AND HEATING TOOLS

Mini-tool or Dremel tool

Mini-tools usually have an assortment of interchangeable heads so you can use them for a variety of tasks, from cutting away unwanted metal to sanding and polishing disks. This is a definitely a handy tool to have in your tool collection.

Drill

A small electric drill is useful to drill holes in harder materials. Mark the position first with a center punch (see page 15).

Heat gun

For heating Friendly Plastic so that it becomes pliable. You can also use a heat gun to color copper, though this method will take longer than if you use a butane torch.

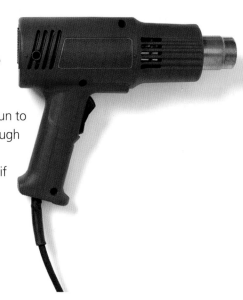

Butane torch

A small butane torch is used for soldering and for annealing (see page 33) metal before hammering. There are many types out there; I use one that is designed for precious metal clay. You can also use an inexpensive propane torch.

Soldering iron

For soldering metals using a solder with a low melting point.

ADHESIVE, RESIN, AND SOLDER

Silicone-based adhesive

E-6000® is a silicone-based glue useful for attaching components together. It dries clear but needs to be used with proper ventilation.

Mod Podge®

(not shown)

Basic white craft glue that is used with paper and dries clear. It can also be used as a sealer. Note that it is not waterproof.

Two-part casting resin

A casting material that comes in two parts: The resin and the hardener. I use resin whenever I want a durable glossy finish or when I want to embed objects. It is transparent when it cures.

Solder *(not shown)*
Used to join metal components together permanently. Solder comes in several forms: Plumber's solder can be found at a local hardware (DIY) store and can be used with copper or brass; sterling silver requires silver solder, which comes in sheets, wire, or chips.

Flux *(not shown)*
Necessary when using solder because it helps this to flow smoothly and to go where you want it.

Tip *Silver solder is available in a variety of melting points: hard, medium, and easy. If soldering several pieces of silver onto one object, begin with the highest melting point and graduate to a lower one. This way, your soldered pieces will not come apart as you add additional pieces.*

CLAMPS AND VICES

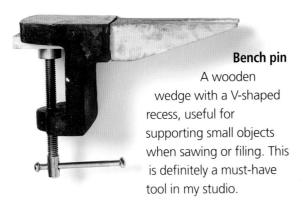

Bench pin
A wooden wedge with a V-shaped recess, useful for supporting small objects when sawing or filing. This is definitely a must-have tool in my studio.

Third hand
A very useful adjustable clamp with two jaws, which can both be positioned to hold small pieces exactly where you need them.

Bench vice *(not shown)*
Clamps onto the bench to hold small items securely.

Adjustable-head vice
Similar to a bench vice, but has a head that can be placed at different angles.

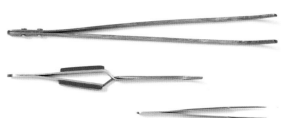

Tweezers and tongs
To hold and position very small components. Use only copper or bamboo tongs when working with pickle (see page 18).

FINISHING, SMOOTHING, AND POLISHING TOOLS

Brass brush
This brush is for cleaning up metal and adding polished highlights to textured areas.

Sandpaper
Different grades are available—use 400-grit for fine work. Sandpaper also produces a nice matte finish on the surface.

Files
These come in different sizes and shapes and are useful for deburring edges of sawn metal as well as for reforming the shape. The two files that I use most often are the flat hand file and the half round—useful in sanding rounded areas. Smaller needle files are useful for detail work. Files can also provide a nice surface texture.

> **Tips** *When filing, apply pressure on the forward motion instead of sawing back and forth—this will make the most of your energy and prolong the life of your file.*
> *Keep a file brush around and give your files a quick sweep on a regular basis to keep them clean and sharp.*

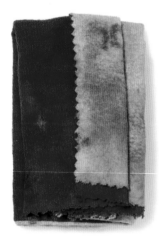

Polishing cloth
A cloth impregnated with rouge to buff metal up to a very high shine.

Liver of sulfur *(not shown)*
My absolute favorite finish, liver of sulfur is used to add patina to metal. Mix according to manufacturer's directions and use in a well-ventilated area since it gives off a foul odor similar to rotten eggs. The hotter and stronger the solution, the quicker it will turn metal to a gunmetal color.

Pickle *(not shown)*
A mild sulfuric acid solution used to clean metal before and after soldering. Use copper or bamboo tongs to remove pieces from the pickle bath—do not use steel materials, as these will have a chemical reaction to the bath.

Materials

Stringing materials

Leather cord
Available in a small selection of colors and several different thicknesses.

Ribbons
There are so many different ribbons on the market that the choice is almost endless; they give a softer, more delicate look than you usually get when using chain.

Fabrics
Several projects in the book use strips of fabric, which can be torn from any woven textile. Scraps of linen or recycled denim from a old pair of jeans are good choices.

Chains
There is a wide variety of chains available, in a range of finishes and with many different sizes and shapes of link.

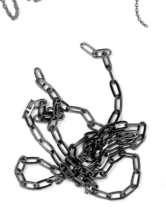

Sheet metals

Copper

Copper sheet is easy to work and its warm color adds an attractive glow to any metalwork. It comes in a variety of thicknesses and may be colored with heat, creating a rainbow of colors. Because it is relatively inexpensive and very versatile, it is my main choice of metal to work with.

Brass

More yellow in color than copper, brass is ideal used as a contrast to copper or silver. It also comes in a variety of thicknesses.

Aluminum

A silvery metal that is a good substitute for sterling silver, where you want the look but not the cost.

Pewter

A very soft, silvery-gray metal that is ideal for some types of jewelry-making. I use ArtEmboss®, which comes in a sheet about the size of a piece of paper. It is very creamy, accepts texture very well, and cuts easily with scissors. It is also a great substitute for some silver, since it will not tarnish.

Sterling silver

A precious metal, silver is quite expensive to buy but adds a special look to jewelry. Scraps can be returned to the foundry and sold back for recycling.

Found objects

All kinds of small items can be used in jewelry—either those found around the home or purchased especially for the task. Dig out your old keys, bottlecaps, buttons, and so on. As long as it's not too heavy or extremely large, you can use it in jewelry.

General findings and beads

General jewelry-making elements—such as head pins, jump rings, clasps, and eyelets—are all used for assembling pieces. These are just a small sampling of the basics I have continuously in my studio.

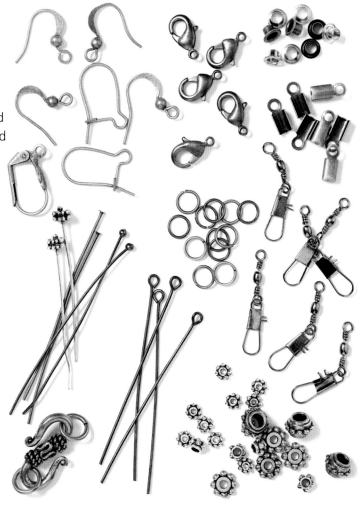

Wires and tubes

Wire

Wire used for jewelry making is generally silver, brass, copper, aluminum, or galvanized steel. It is available in different gauges—a higher number indicates a thinner wire. I purchase the majority of my thicker-gauge wires in the hardware store. I also drop the entire spool in liver of sulfur solution before using it, since this saves me time later.

Copper tubes

Tubes can be sliced into sections, curved, or flattened. Copper tubing is the most common and is available in many diameters.

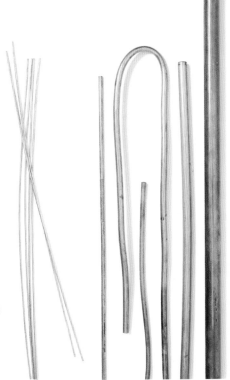

Techniques

To me, this is probably the most important chapter in the book; in learning techniques you increase your skill level and open up a whole world of possibilities. There are so many metalworking techniques available that it can get a bit overwhelming, but I've chosen to highlight a few of my favorites when designing the projects in this book. Familiarize yourself with these and don't be too hard on yourself as you learn these new skills. Remember, practice makes perfect.

OPENING AND CLOSING A JUMP RING

1 Grasp the jump ring with pliers on each side of the slit. Gently twist the ends in opposite directions until the slit opens.

2 After you haved added elements, close the jump ring by repeating the twisting action in reverse to bring the ends back together neatly.

Tip *Don't open a jump ring by pulling the ends apart, because this will distort the shape and it will be hard to get it back into a perfect circle. By opening it in the way shown here, the jump ring will stay perfectly round. You can solder the slit shut if desired to prevent the jump ring from opening again in the future.*

MAKING JUMP RINGS

1 Wind the wire around a ring mandrel or any other circular object that is the desired circumference of the jump ring.

2 Slide the wire spiral off the rod and then snip the coils into separate rings using wire cutters.

MAKING A BALL END ON STERLING SILVER WIRE

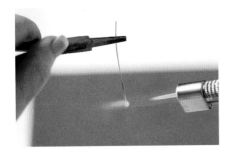

1 Hold the wire vertically with pliers and heat the end with a torch flame. As the wire begins to glow, a ball of melted metal will form at the end, traveling upward and getting larger as it takes in more metal. Remove the flame before the ball becomes so heavy that it falls off. The heavier the gauge of wire, the bigger the ball you can create.

CREATING A DECORATIVE EARRING WIRE

1 Cut a short piece of wire approximately 2in. (5cm) long. Hammer one end flat.

2 Use round-nose pliers to curve the flattened end round to create a loop.

3 Use bail-making pliers or a dowel rod to create a large loop. Snip off excess wire and file the ends smooth.

MAKING AN S-CLASP AND LOOP

1 Working directly off the spool, create a very slight bend in the wire. Bend the wire around the bail-making pliers in the opposite direction to create the first curve.

2 Bend the wire around again in the opposite direction, creating the second curve and finishing the "S" shape. Cut the end from the spool and bend this end around into a ring. File the ends smooth if necessary.

3 Wrap a length of thinner wire around the middle of the middle of the loop to embellish, if desired.

4 Place the S-shape on the bench block and tap gently with a hammer to flatten and harden the metal (see work hardening and annealing metal on page 33).

5 Working from the spool again, bend the wire into a small loop approximately 1½in. (4cm) from the end of the wire. Wrap the "free" end of wire around the loop a couple of times and cut off the excess. Still working from the spool, create a larger loop and finish by wrapping the end of the wire around the base of the large loop. Cut the wire from the spool and file the ends smooth. Attach the S-clasp and loop to the stringing material with a jump ring.

MAKING A HOOK

1 Cut a short piece of wire approximately 4in. (10cm) long and fold it in two, leaving a long end on one side.

2 Pinch the folded end together, using flat-nose pliers.

3 Use round-nose pliers to create a loop on the shorter end.

4 Wrap the longer end around the shorter one just below the loop, and then trim off any excess wire.

5 Bend the doubled end around, using round-nose pliers to create the hook.

6 To finish, slightly curve the tip of the hook upward.

CREATING A BEADED DANGLE

1 Thread the chosen beads and spacer beads onto a head pin.

2 Use round-nose pliers to curve the top of the headpin into a loop, centering the loop over the beads. Cut off any excess head pin.

CREATING A BEADED LINK

1 Create your own eye pin by cutting a length of wire and creating a loop at the end with round-nose pliers, or use a suitable store-bought eye pin instead.

2 Thread beads and spacer beads onto the wire in the desired order. Snip off the excess wire, leaving ¼–½in. (5–12mm) remaining.

3 Using round-nose pliers, curve the end of the wire into a loop as close in size as possible to the one at the other end.

4 Adjust the two loops, centering them over the beads and the line of the wire.

BRASS BRUSHING

This is a polishing technique that can create a soft matte surface on metals. It is also a useful way of removing unwanted residue from tiny areas and brightening the surface.

1 Place the object on a rubber surface and brush the bristles of a brass brush across it—the rubber surface helps to hold the item in place and prevent it from sliding.

2 Finish off by polishing up the surface of the item with a soft cloth.

TEXTURING THE SURFACE

Lots of objects can be used to texture the surface of soft metal—look for unusual things to pound into the metal to create interesting effects.

1 Place the metal on a bench block. Using a ball-pein hammer, strike the metal with the round end to create tiny dents until the desired patterning has been achieved.

2 Turn the piece over and gently tap it flat again, this time using the flat end of the hammer.

DECOUPAGE

1 Apply decoupage glue to the front of the metal piece. Place a torn piece of vintage paper on the metal surface and apply glue over the top of paper. Allow to dry.

2 You can add more vintage appeal by rubbing the surface of the paper with rubber-stamping inks.

USING RESIN

1 Follow all the manufacturer's instructions for mixing the resin—generally it is equal parts of hardener and resin.

2 Stir the mix for several minutes. At this point, it is ready to be poured into or on top of the desired object.

USING RUB 'N' BUFF® TO ADD AN EASY PATINA

1 Use a small sponge to apply a little Rub 'N' Buff® over the surface of the metal piece. Allow to dry slightly.

2 Buff away some of the polish with a soft cloth, until you have achieved the finish you want.

USING LIVER OF SULFUR TO ADD PATINA

Tip *Use the liver of sulfur mixture in a very well ventilated area as it is very stinky—it smells like rotten eggs!*

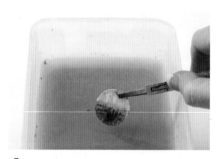

1 Drop a couple of nuggets of liver of sulfur into very warm/slightly hot water and allow them to dissolve completely. The stronger the solution and the hotter the water, the faster this will create a deep gunmetal patina. Dip the finished item in the solution until the desired finished has been achieved.

2 After adding the patina, rinse and dry the item. You can then brass brush or polish up selected areas if necessary, to highlight the contrast in areas of pattern.

USING AMMONIA TO ADD BLUE PATINA

Fold a piece of mesh along the sides to create a rack and place this inside a plastic container. Mix the ammonia solution: 2 parts water, 1 part ammonia, and a tablespoon of salt. Pour into the container to just below the rack. Dip the metal piece into the solution and lay it on the mesh rack. Sprinkle the metal with a little salt. Seal the box and leave for a couple of hours—the patina will develop from a light to an intense blue. Remove the metal and allow to dry.

Tip *The fumes from the ammonia/salt mix are noxious, so be very sure only to mix and use it in a very well ventilated area. Store the solution in a box with a secure, snap-close lid. This mix will work on both copper and brass.*

ETCHING USING FERRIC CHLORIDE

Following the manufacturer's directions, mix the solution in a glass or plastic bowl with a lid—do not use metal. Always pour the chemical into the water.

1 Create the resist by stamping a design onto the metal with a rubber stamp and ink. You could also draw the design in permanent marker. Outline stickers and rub-on transfers also provide a great resist and come in a variety of different patterns and lettering styles.

2 Coat the entire back of the metal piece with permanent marker or nail enamel. Place the metal in the etching solution and leave until the desired depth of etch has been achieved. Depending on the strength of the solution this may take one to several hours, so check frequently.

3 Remove the metal from the etching solution and rinse. Patinas may now be applied to bring out the patterns in the metal.

SETTING A SAW BLADE

  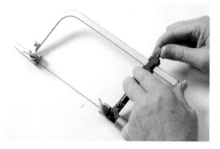

1 Make sure the new blade is facing down and outward. Undo the finger screw and insert the blade into the slot at the top of the saw. Tighten the screw again.

2 Undo the finger screw at the bottom of the saw and place the other end of the blade in the slot. Tighten the screw to hold the blade securely in place.

3 Press downward on the lower section of the saw while pressing upward on the top section. Tighten the back screw. The blade should be tight and will "ping" when plucked if correctly inserted.

CUTTING METAL SHAPES WITH A SAW

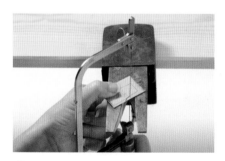  

1 Mark the shape on a piece of metal with permanent marker or a scribe. Apply Cut Lube to the saw blade to lubricate it. Lay the metal onto the bench peg. To create the first cut, slightly angle the blade and draw down. Repeat, cutting out the shape by following the marked line.

2 File away any rough edges all around the shape and round off any very sharp corners with a metal file.

3 A dremel tool or small hobby drill that is equipped with a grinding bit can be used to speed up the smoothing process.

FORMING A SHAPE

1 Place the metal piece to be shaped into a suitable recess in a dapping block. Place the matching wooden punch over the top and tap the end with the round end of a hammer to shape the piece into a curved dome. This technique can also be used with metal dapping blocks and matching punches.

CUTTING COPPER TUBING

1 Open up the jaws of the tube cutter and slip the tubing inside. Tighten the jaws again so that the tubing fits firmly into the tube cutter.

2 Twist the cutter around the tube until you have cut right through the metal. Tighten the jaws a little more after every couple of turns. Snap the ring off the end of the tube.

MAKING A HOLE

1 Place the point of the punch against the metal and strike the other end with a large hammer to make a small hole.

2 If you do not have a punch, you can use a large, sharp nail instead.

SETTING AN EYELET

Tip *When setting eyelets into fabric or paper you generally use a special tool, which spreads the reverse of the eyelet into a "flower" shape on the back of the work to hold it in place. When setting an eyelet into metal this is not necessary—the metal of the eyelet compresses evenly around the hole, so it gives the visual effect of an industrial rivet.*

1 Drill the hole for the eyelet and push it into place.

2 Place the metal on a bench block and hammer the eyelet to set it.

BASIC SOLDERING WITH A BUTANE TORCH

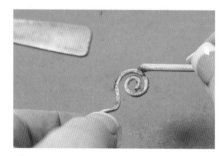

1 Clean and pickle the pieces of metal to be soldered. Apply a little flux only to the exact areas that will be soldered.

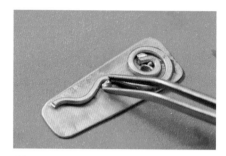

2 Working on a heat-protected surface—such as a firebrick or ceramic tile—place the two pieces of metal together so that they touch. Cut a few chips of solder with scissors and place them around the join.

3 Turn on the torch and begin heating up the metal as evenly as possible. Do not hold the flame directly on one area.

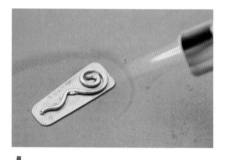

4 As the metal begins to heat to the right temperature, the chips of solder will start to melt into blobs.

5 When the solder reaches the appropriate temperature, it will completely melt and run along the fluxed area.

Tips *To prevent the solder from running into undesired areas, draw a line with a lead pencil around the area—the solder will not run across the lead.*

Solder is drawn to heat, so sometimes it helps to heat from the opposite side.

SOLDERING ON A JUMP RING WITH A SOLDER IRON

1 Prepare the piece to be soldered. Here the solder is being smoothed and melted with the tip of the iron before the jump ring is added.

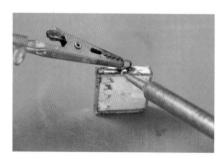

2 Add a jump ring to the top of the desired piece, using a third hand for support. Allow the solder to cool before removing the third hand.

WORK HARDENING AND ANNEALING METAL

When you bend a piece of wire or metal back and forth several times it becomes work hardened, which can make it very brittle and cause it to snap. To prevent this you need to anneal it, which is the process of softening the metal back to its flexible state, making it much easier to work with. This process can be done in two different ways.

Apply paste flux to the metal that you wish to anneal. Once the flux is heated with a torch and turns clear, the metal is annealed. Quench it in pickle solution and rinse—you will notice that the metal is now a muted pink color. You can also anneal metal by holding it in a flame until it comes to a light glow—do this under a dim light and you will notice a yellow back flame. Remove the heat and quench the metal in pickle, then rinse.

Tips *Annealing makes all metal easier to form and bend, especially when working with larger gauges of wire and thicker metals.*

Metal can be annealed over and over again to prevent it from cracking or breaking.

Hammering metal—to texture or form it into shapes—hardens it and makes it stronger, up to a point. Over-hardening will make the metal brittle.

USING PICKLE

Pickle is a dry acid concentrate used to remove oxides (fire stain) from the surface of metal after soldering. It works quickest when warm. Cleaning with pickle is a necessary step when soldering metals because solder will not adhere well to dirty, oily metal. Make up the pickle solution in a glass bowl according to the manufacturer's instructions. Drop the metal shape into the pickle solution until the surface has cleaned up, which generally takes a couple of minutes. Use pickling tongs to remove the metal.

CHAPTER 2
Creating the Look

In this chapter you will learn a few of the basics of jewelry making to get you started. All these projects are quite easy to make, but the results will be stunning and will help build confidence in your metalworking skills. Don't be afraid to experiment and combine elements from different projects to create your own individual designs.

Floral Garden

This project is the ideal introduction to making your own jewelry; it simply uses purchased elements, joined together with jump rings, to acquaint you with basic jewelry-making techniques. The flowers are scrapbooking brads—look around your local craft store to see what else you may be able to use in this way.

1 Arrange the flower brads and dangles on the work surface to create the necklace design. Move them around until you are happy with the positioning.

MATERIALS

Set of 6 antique-effect flower brads

3 pre-made pearl dangles

2 pre-made pearl bead links

Hand punch

18 antique finish jump rings or split rings

1 x 1¼-in. (3-cm) lengths of antique-effect chain

2 x 3-in. (7.5-cm) length of antique-effect chain

Round-nose or bail-making pliers

Antique-finish lobster clasp

2 If further holes are required in the brads to create the layout, pierce these with a hand punch.

3 Choose the color bead brad for the center of each flower. Thread the brad through the hole at the center of the flower and open out the arms at the back. Repeat for the other flowers.

4 Join sections together using the jump rings (see page 22). Attach one end of each 1¼in. (3cm) chain to the flowers on either side. Add the pre-made bead link. Attach a chain to each end of the necklace to create the desired length. Attach the clasp to the ends of the chains.

Tips *This project uses purchased dangles and bead links, but if you want to make up your own unique versions, see the instructions on page 26. Broken jewelry is a great source of elements that can easily be recycled into exciting new designs.*

Time Traveler

Here the rather industrial-looking inner workings of a watch are combined with delicate filigree and an elegant dragonfly to create a delicate and romantic pendant. The ribbon adds softness to the total effect, but this design would look equally charming on an antique chain.

1 Place the filigree finding on a rubber work surface and brush with the wire brush to distress the surface and give it an antique look. Polish up with a soft cloth.

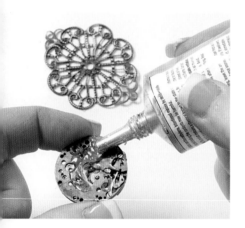

2 Place a large dab of glue onto the back of the watch workings and place it on the filigree finding in the desired position.

MATERIALS
Circular filigree finding
Brass wire brush
Rubber mat
Polishing cloth
Interior workings of a watch
Silicone-based glue
Brass dragonfly charm finding
Rub 'N' Buff® (optional)
Head pin
Bead
Spacer bead
Round-nose pliers
2 large jump rings
2yd (2m) ribbon
Scissors

Tip *Look around flea markets, thrift (charity) shops, and yard (car boot) sales for old, non-working watches that you can take apart and use for jewelry making.*

3 If necessary, follow the instructions for the Rub 'N' Buff® patina on page 28 to add patina to the dragonfly charm. Attach the dragonfly with glue over the watch workings.

4 Thread the bead and the spacer bead onto a head pin. Use round-nose pliers to curve the top of the head pin into a loop, centering the loop over the beads. Cut off any excess wire. Add this dangle to the base of the necklace using a jump ring.

5 Add a jump ring to the top of the necklace, as described on page 22. Fold the ribbon in half and thread the double length through the jump ring. Snip through at the fold and then tie the ribbon into a pretty bow to fasten the necklace.

Old World Earrings

Copper and turquoise go really well together; the patina on copper has a blue-green tinge that picks up the color of the stone. I have shaped the metal pieces into a slight curve to soften their geometric look—this is easy to do and is a technique that will be extended in later projects.

MATERIALS

0.025 (22-gauge) copper sheet
Jeweler's saw
Bench block
Cut Lube
Ball-pein hammer
Hand file or mini electric file
Rub 'N' Buff® Patina
Polishing cloth
Punch or sharp nail
Wooden dapping block and punches
4 turquoise beads
2 head pins
Round-nose pliers
2 jump rings
Pair of earring wires

1 Cut out two earring shapes using the template on page 125. File the edges smooth and round the corners. Place the metal piece on the work surface and use the rounded end of the ball-pein hammer to texture the surface. Turn over and hammer the shape flat again.

2 Patina the surface with a little Rub 'N' Buff® (see the technique on page 28).

3 Use a punch or nail as described on page 31 to make a small hole at the top end of the shape for the earring wire. Shape the copper piece into a gentle curve using the wooden dapping block (see the technique on page 31).

4 Create a dangle with two turquoise beads and a head pin, as described on page 26. Wrap the end of the wire around the top a few times to create an attractive effect.

5 Assemble the earrings using jump rings. Repeat all the steps to make the second matching earring.

Tip *Recycled copper flashing from a roof is an excellent material to use—you can take advantage of the natural patina created by Mother Nature instead of using Rub 'N' Buff®.*

Copper Cuff

By sandwiching thin copper sheets with double stick tape and "sewing" on the copper wire, you can achieve the look of a formed and soldered copper cuff without any metalworking or soldering. This is an ideal project to try if you are not yet confident enough to use a butane torch to solder and this thinner copper sheet is easy to work with.

MATERIALS

Two 8 x 3in. (20 x 7.5cm) ArtEmboss® copper medium sheets

Double stick tape

Sharpie marker

Scissors

Hand punch

Bench block

Butane torch or lighter

Hammer

WireForm® thin copper rods

Bail-making pliers

Silver-colored wire

Rub 'N' Buff® Patina

Bracelet mandrel (optional)

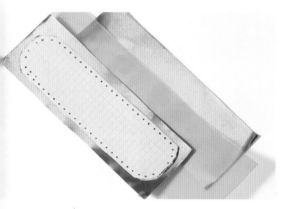

1 Sandwich double-stick tape between two 8 x 3-in. (20 x 7.5-cm) pieces of copper sheet. Use the template on page 124 and draw the shape of the bracelet with the marker. Mark the holes to be punched with the marker.

2 Cut out the cuff shape with heavy-duty scissors. Pierce each stitching hole around the edge using the hand punch.

4 Attach the copper rods to the cuff by "stitching" through the holes with the silver-colored wire. Shape the cuff into a bracelet with your hands or against a bracelet mandrel. Rub with Rub 'N' Buff® to add patina to the texture.

3 Play the flame of the torch over the cuff to change the color of the copper surface. Texture the surface of the cuff with the hammer. Anneal the copper rods (see page 33) and then bend to shape them around the outer edge of the template, creating a spiral at each end.

Tips

Change the look of this bracelet by varying the width of the cuff.

To fit a larger wrist, add length to the center of template before using it to mark out the cuff.

Faerie Punk Bangle

There is a very wide range of ready-made findings available and combining these is a wonderful way to make up jewelry quickly. You don't have to use them just as they come—experiment with different ways of adding patina or color, and with combining elements in different ways.

1 Carefully following the instructions on page 29, make up the ammonia/salt mix and add the fairy shape to turn it bright blue-green. Leave it in the solution until you have achieved the desired depth of color. Sand off some of the green patina.

MATERIALS

Ammonia
Water
Salt
Plastic container with lid
Purchased copper fairy finding
400-grit sandpaper
Red alcohol-based ink
Cosmetic sponge
Watch workings
Silicone-based glue
Purchased copper bangle

2 Highlight some areas with a little bright color alcohol-based ink to give an iridescent look to the fairy's wings.

3 Add the watch workings to the front of the fairy using a fairly large dab of the silicone-based glue.

4 Glue the fairy ensemble to the front of the bangle—move it around until you get the desired position. Prop the bangle up until the glue has set securely.

Half Moon Rising Earrings

These simple etched copper earrings are given extra movement and interest with pretty silver dangles that catch the light. They require some cutting skills, but otherwise are very easy to make. You could add beads or charms instead of the silver dangles for a different look, or to add some color to the design.

1 Cut a copper rectangle and etch a design following the instructions on page 29. Position the disk cutter over the etched sheet so that the smaller circle is slightly closer to the top, leaving enough around the edge to cut the outer circle. Insert the corresponding punch and hammer until the disk pops out the bottom. Cut the larger circle around the hole of the smaller one. Repeat to create a second earring disk. File and sand the edges smooth.

MATERIALS

3-in. (7.5-cm) square of 0.025 (22-gauge) copper sheet

Jeweler's saw

Cut Lube

Pigment-based ink pad

Rubberstamp with choice design

Liver of sulfur

Ferric chloride etching solution

Disk cutter

Hammer

Files

400-grit sandpaper

Bench block

Center punch

Drill

Dapping block and punches

20-gauge silver wire

Wire cutters

Round-nose pliers

Bail-making pliers

Pair of earring wires

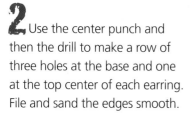

2 Use the center punch and then the drill to make a row of three holes at the base and one at the top center of each earring. File and sand the edges smooth.

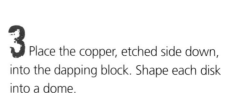

3 Place the copper, etched side down, into the dapping block. Shape each disk into a dome.

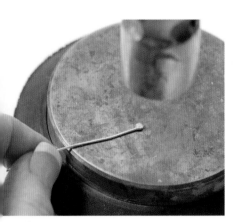

4 Cut three lengths of silver wire for each earring, two around ¾in. (18mm) long and one 1in. (2.5cm) long. Flatten one end of each by hammering it on a bench block.

5 Curve the top of one of the longer dangles into a loop and attach to the center base of the copper disk. Add the shorter dangles on each side. Add the earring wire to the top. Repeat on the other earring.

Hanging My Heart Necklace

Hearts in various forms are a staple of jewelry making, but adding a little distortion to the standard shape gives it more of an edge. The inserted eyelet and the wire wrapping give this design a contemporary, industrial, steampunk feel.

MATERIALS

3in. (7.5cm) square of 0.025 (22-gauge) copper sheet
Permanent marker
Center punch
Drill
Jeweler's saw
Cut Lube
Files
400-grit sandpaper
Bench block
³⁄₁₆in. (4.5mm) copper eyelet
Hammer
Nail set or metal stamp of choice
20-gauge gold wire
Round-nose pliers
Small brass nut
Bead
18-gauge copper wire
Pencil
Leather cord
1 jump ring
Fastener of choice

1 Using the template on page 125, copy the double heart shape onto the sheet of copper.

2 Mark a hole with the center punch and then drill a hole at the edge of the inside heart where indicated on the template.

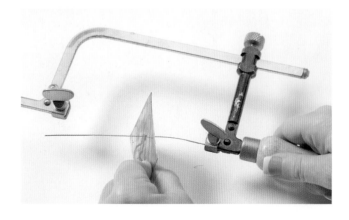

3 Undo the saw blade on the jeweler's saw at one end and insert the saw blade through the hole just made. Secure the end of the blade to the saw again.

4 Cut out around the center heart—you can save it and use it for another project. Cut out around the outer heart.

5 File the edges smooth and then finish with sandpaper. Drill the hole for the eyelet and set it in place (see technique on page 31). Add texture across the surface with the metal stamp. Wrap a short length of gold wire around the base of the heart. Create a dangle (see technique on page 26) with the bead and nut and hang from the gold coil.

6 Coil the copper wire around a pencil and thread through several strands of leather cording. Attach the heart to the coil with a jump ring. Finish the ends of the leather cord by wire wrapping and creating a loop end. Add the fastener of choice.

Tricolor Droplet Earrings

This is such a basic design, but it lends itself to many variations. Using three different metals immediately creates extra interest—but for an even simpler version you could use the same metal for each disk. You could also try adding different textures or patinas to make the disks look different.

1 Using the disk cutter, cut two disks from each metal sheet in decreasing sizes. Mark with a center punch and then drill a hole at the top and bottom of the two largest disks and at the top only of the smallest. File all the edges smooth. Sand the surface of each disk smooth.

2 Use the dapping block to form the disks into domes.

3 Polish the surface to a high shine, using a polishing cloth. Attach the disks together with jump rings. Attach the earring wires using the jump rings.

MATERIALS

- 3-in. (7.5-cm) square of 0.015 (26-gauge) brass sheet
- 2-in. (5-cm) square of 0.015 (26-gauge) copper sheet
- 1-in. (2.5-cm) square of 26-gauge sterling silver sheet
- Disk cutter
- Hammer
- Center punch
- Drill
- Files
- 400-grit sandpaper
- Dapping block and punches
- Polishing cloth
- 4 jump rings
- Pair of earring wires
- Bail-making pliers

Tip *For a different look, try assembling the earrings in the opposite order, with the smallest disk at the top. Remember to drill only one hole in the largest disk, and two in both the other two disks.*

Time Warp Necklace

This necklace was inspired by those melting clocks in the paintings of Salvador Dali—the elongated shape of the pendant echoes the warped and elongated clock faces. I like the idea that time and space can be distorted—particularly when, as ever, I am short of both!

MATERIALS

Permanent marker
Cardstock
Scissors
Double-stick tape
ArtEmboss® pewter medium sheet
Ball-pein hammer
Bench block
Rub 'N' Buff® Ebony
Cosmetic sponge
Polishing cloth
WireForm® thin copper rods
Metal cutters
24-gauge copper wire
Round-nose pliers
Bail-making pliers
ArtEmboss® copper medium sheet
Hand punch
2 brass brads
WireForm® thin brass rods
Clock face charm
Silicone-based glue
Leather cord
20-gauge silver wire or leather cord

1 Using the base template on page 125, cut out one shape from the cardstock. Place the cardstock shape on double-stick tape and cut out. Remove the tape backing and place the shape face down on the pewter. Cut out the shape.

2 Soften the edges by rubbing them with the side of the marker to smooth them over the cardstock.

3 Texture the surface using the end of the ball-pein hammer. Rub a little Rub 'N' Buff® over the surface to highlight the design. Apply double-stick tape to the back of the design.

Tip *The cardstock used for this project does not have to be anything special, as you will not be able to see it when the necklace is finished. Recycled cardboard from a cereal box would work just fine.*

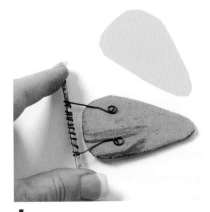

4 Cut a 1½-in. (4-cm) length of thin copper rod and hammer flat. Wrap this bar with 24-gauge copper wire, leaving long ends. Curl the ends into spirals and place these over the cardstock side of the pendant. Remove the backing from the double stick tape and press on the coiled ends. Apply a layer of pewter sheet over the top and cut out flush. Soften the edges, as before.

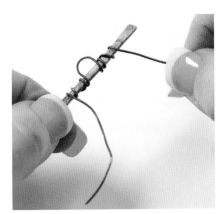

5 Cut a 1-in. (2.5-cm) length of thin copper rod and hammer flat. Wrap with 24-gauge copper wire, making a larger hanging loop in the middle and leaving long ends. Wrap the ends around the bar attached to the pendant to secure.

6 Cut out the copper shape using the inset template on page 125. Use a hand punch to add a hole and attach the brads. Hammer two 2-in. (5-cm) lengths of brass rod flat. Assemble and glue the copper shape, brass strips, and clock face on top of the pewter pendant, using the photograph above as a guide. Finish the leather cord ends as described on page 49, or use leather cord findings, and add the hanging cord.

Rootbeer Float Necklace

This project makes use of the design and color of soda cans—and recycling is right in fashion with all ages. Look out for interesting cans to use; there is a wide range of possible types that can be used for this project, but I have chosen rootbeer cans for their rich, golden-brown tones.

MATERIALS

2 or 3 aluminum soda cans in colors/designs of your choice

Stylus

Texture folder (optional)

Pasta machine (optional)

Scissors or wire cutters

400-grit sandpaper

¾in. (2cm) round circle punch

Files

Double-stick tape

Ball-pein hammer

⅛in. (3mm) hole punch or drill

28 brass eyelets

28 brass jump rings

14 swivels with pins from a fishing supply store

Round-nose pliers

Bail-making pliers

8in. (20cm) natural brass chain

2 oval decorative links

2 x 3½-in. (8-cm) sections of natural brass chain

2 large brass jump rings

Brass lobster clasp

1 Cut the tops and bottoms off the aluminum cans, cut down the side, and flatten the cans out into sheets. Texture the metal with a stylus, or put through a pasta machine with the texture folder.

2 Turn the metal over and sand the raised side slightly to highlight areas of the design. Cut out 56 circles using the ¾in. (2cm) round circle punch. Stick them back to back to make double-sided disks. Sand off any sharp edges, if necessary.

3 Punch or drill a hole in the top edge of each disk. Set a brass eyelet in each hole, following the instructions on page 31. Use swivel pins and jump rings to attach the disks in pairs, spacing them evenly on the 8-in. (20-cm) length chain.

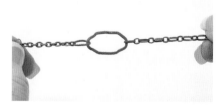

4 Add the large links to each end of the chain via jump rings. Attach a shorter length of chain on each side. Add the clasp to the ends of the chains.

Tip *The texture here was created by running the metal with an embossing folder through the pasta machine, but you can just draw a pattern on the metal can with a wooden stylus. Or you may choose to have no texture if your soda cans are detailed.*

Sunray Pendant

This project is created using Friendly Plastic® combined with copper and brass to create a unique design full of color. Friendly Plastic® is ideal to create your own artifacts and aged elements, because it is easy to add color, shape, and texture to create just the piece you need.

1 Cut a small section of Friendly Plastic® and color the surface with the alcohol-based inks and the Patina Rub 'N' Buff®. Work on a piece of heatproof material ready for step 2 and to avoid damaging your worktop.

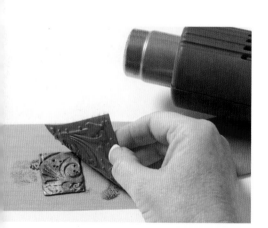

2 Heat up the Friendly Plastic® with a heat gun until it softens slightly—if it begins to bubble, it is too hot. Remove the heat and the bubbles should disappear. Press a texture stamp over the plastic and press to create a texture on the surface.

3 Add a little Gold Leaf Rub 'N' Buff® over the texture to highlight the design. Cut the Friendly Plastic® piece down with scissors to match the inner template on page 125.

MATERIALS

Sheet of matte gold Friendly Plastic®
Scissors
Alcohol-based inks
Rub 'N' Buff® in Patina and Gold Leaf
Cosmetic sponge
Heatproof firebrick or ceramic tile
Heat gun
Texture stamp
2-in. (5-cm) square of 0.025 (22-gauge) copper sheet
Jeweler's saw
Cut Lube
24-gauge brass wire
Wire cutters
Round-nose pliers
Bail-making pliers
Ball-pein hammer
Bench block
Silicone-based glue
Center punch
Drill
WireForm® thin brass rod
24-gauge copper wire
Leader cord necklace

Tip *This pendant is shown on a leather cord, but it would also look perfect on the Silver Halo Choker on page 62.*

4 Cut a piece of copper sheet using the outer template on page 125. Cut a 1-in. (2.5-cm) length of brass wire, create a few curves in the length and then flatten with the hammer. Assemble the pendant using silicone-based glue and following the photograph, right. Drill one hole on either side at the top.

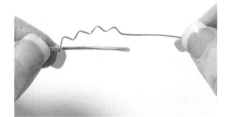

5 Cut a 1¼-in. (3-cm) length of thin brass rod and hammer it flat to make a bar. Wrap the bar with 24-gauge brass wire, making a larger hanging loop in the middle. Then wrap the bar with copper wire, leaving long ends. Take the copper ends through the holes in the pendant and then back to wrap and attach in place.

Material Girl

This project uses simple embroidery stitching, but blanket stitch is really easy to work. You could use an over hand stitch instead—look in a sewing book for some alternative ideas. Since you stamp the center panel using individual letters, you can write any word or name that you like.

MATERIALS

¾ x 3-in. (1 x 7.5-cm) piece of ArtEmboss® aluminum medium sheet

Scissors

Files

Hammer

Metal alphabet stamps

Bench block

Black acrylic paint

Cosmetic sponge

Hand punch

4 silver eyelets/rivets

4 x 6½-in. (6 x 15-cm) piece of denim

2 x 6½-in. (3 x 15-cm) piece of felt

Ivory/off-white embroidery floss

Embroidery needle

2 tabs from a soda can

2 buttons

24-gauge steel wire

Round-nose pliers

Bail-making pliers

3 jump rings

Charms of choice

1 Round the corners of the aluminum piece, and file the edges smooth. Hammer in letters to create words of your choice. Apply black paint, removing the excess but allowing paint to remain in the grooves. Punch a hole in each corner of the tag and set eyelets, as described on page 31.

2 Cut out two pieces of denim and one piece of felt, using the template on page 124. Sandwich the felt between the layers of denim. Blanket stitch around the edges in the embroidery floss to join the layers together.

3 Sew the aluminum tag onto the fabric cuff using embroidery floss and working in over hand stitch.

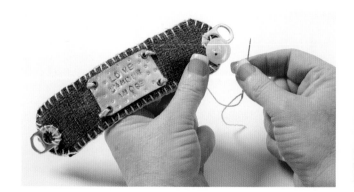

4 Sew the soda can tabs onto the ends of the cuff. Sew a button over each of the tabs. Create an S-clasp hook (see page 24) in steel wire and attach to one of the tabs with a jump ring.

Tips *When stamping the words, mark the centerline and draw lines for the words in ink. Work outward from the middle to get everything centered correctly. Remove the ink at the end either by sanding or using a dab of acetone.*

For a quicker project, use a purchased ready-made blank fabric or leather cuff.

5 Attach charms to the cuff with jump rings.

CHAPTER 3
Wirework and Found Objects

In this chapter we look at new ways to use found objects, often combining them with wire to tie them together. Wire is an excellent way to add a touch of mystique and antiquity to your designs. Gather your objects and let's begin to explore...

Silver Halo Choker

This basic choker is a staple in my wardrobe. It can be worn alone or you can create a selection of different pendants to slide on to match different outfits, making it very versatile and interchangeable. Make several in different metal colors and widths to add an extra versatility to your designs.

1 Working from the center out, begin flattening the wire against the bench block with the flat end of the hammer. Try to apply the same amount of pressure with each stroke to flatten evenly.

MATERIALS

18in. (45cm) x 14-gauge sterling silver round or half- round wire (dead soft)

Ball-pein hammer

Bench block

Files

Polishing cloth

2 Round the ends of the flattened wire with a file until they are smooth.

3 Create texture along the length of the choker with the back of the ball-pein hammer.

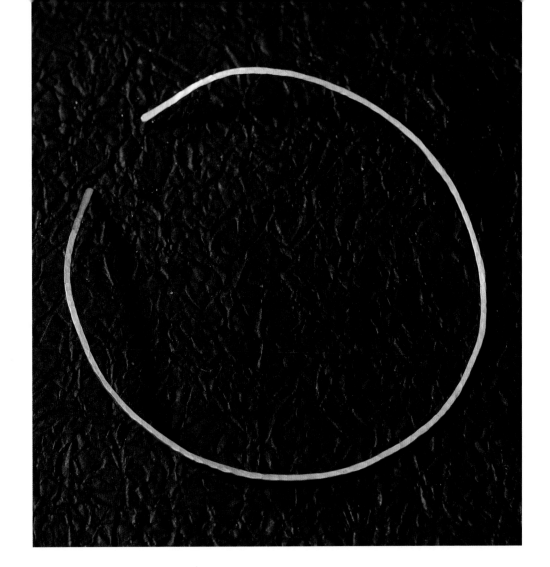

4 Gently massage the ends of the wire to bend into a natural curve to fit around the neck. Polish with a polishing cloth to bring to a shine.

Windsurf Earrings

Soda cans have such great designs when you look at them in detail and the metal is easy to cut and shape, so it is ideal for making jewelry. The shape of these earrings, combined with the branding still visible on the metal, reminded me of windsurf board sails, so I added silver wire spirals to simulate those ideal surfing waves.

1 Cut the top and bottom off the can, cut down the side, and flatten out into a sheet. Use the sail template on page 125 to cut two sails from both the metal can and the aluminum sheet, and the circle punch to stamp out two circles from the metal can only.

sail template on page 125

MATERIALS

Soda cans printed in colors of choice
Scissors
ArtEmboss® aluminum light sheet
¾in. (18mm) circle punch
Double-stick tape
Needle tool
24-gauge non-tarnish silver wire
Wire cutters
Round-nose pliers
Flat-nose pliers
2 beads of choice
Pair of earring wires

2 Apply double-stick tape to the back of one metal can sail and stick it to one of the aluminum sails. Repeat to stick the circle over the sail shape. Make the other earring in the same way.

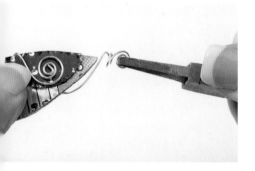

3 Apply texture around the edges, using the tip of the needle tool. Wrap the shape with wire, following the photograph opposite as a guide. Make a loop at the top and a spiral at the base.

4 Thread a bead onto each earring wire. Attach an earring wire to the loop at the top of each earring.

Reflections

A romantic design in glowing copper wire, highlighted with sparkling crystal drops. Chandelier drops are ideal for jewelry, as they are designed to catch the light—and come predrilled with holes. The ball chain makes an interesting change from the more normal link chain.

1 Working off the spool, thread the end of the 20-gauge wire through one hole of the octagonal dangle. Create a loop at the top.

2 Wind the wire around the crystal a few times and then cut off the end, leaving ½in. (12mm). Curl the end into a coil on the front of the crystal. Repeat this step with the other faceted drop.

3 Working off the spool again, bend the wire back approximately 2in. (5cm) from the end and begin creating a teardrop shape from this point, wrapping the wire around several times.

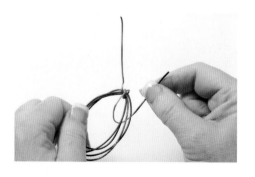

4 Cut the wire from the spool, allowing an extra 4in. (10cm) at the end. Wrap the wire decoratively around the top of the wire teardrop shape a few times to secure it, but do not pull it too tight.

5 Thread the octagonal crystal onto the end of the wire and wrap decoratively to secure it in place.

MATERIALS

20-gauge copper wire

Round-nose pliers

Bail-making pliers

Wire cutters

Crystal octagonal dangle drop from chandelier

Crystal faceted drop from chandelier

Copper-colored ball chain in length desired

Tip *You can embellish the chain with additional charms, made using the directions from the Circle the Globe Bracelet on page 106.*

6 Attach the faceted drop to the center of the teardrop wire shape, using a jump ring made from the same wire.

7 Slide the ball out of the clip to open the end of the ball chain pendant. Slip the pendant onto the chain and then close the fastener again.

Vintage Love Necklace

This design has a real vintage feel, with its old-fashioned key, distressed newsprint, and faceted crystal beads. The leather cord adds to the period look—a contemporary chain would probably have looked out of place.

1 Cut out the copper pendant shape (see page 30) or use a precut copper blank. Glue paper to the front and antique with ink, as described on page 27. Drill a hole at the top and the bottom.

2 Place the key charm on top of the pendant. Wrap with copper wire to hold it in place. Create a dangle (see page 26) using one of the crystal beads. Attach the dangle to the bottom of the pendant.

3 Create two beaded links with a bead cap on each side (see page 26). Thread one loop of the beaded link onto the leather cord. Fold the leather cord upward creating a loop. Wrap firmly with wire to secure. Trim off excess cord. Repeat on the other cord.

MATERIALS

- 0.025 (22-gauge) copper sheet copper sheet or copper pendant blank
- Jeweler's saw
- Cut Lube
- Scrap of newsprint
- Mod Podge® decoupage glue
- Rubberstamping pigment-based inkpad in Vintage Brown
- Soft cloth
- Center punch
- Drill
- Key charm
- 20-gauge copper wire
- Wire cutters
- 3 crystal beads
- 1 head pin
- Round-nose pliers
- Bail-making pliers
- 4 bead caps
- 2 x 6-in. (1.5-cm) leather cord
- Scissors
- Split ring or jump ring

Tip *If you want to make the necklace a little longer after you have already cut the leather cord, just add another S-shape to the ring of the clasp and hook the S-clasp onto this instead to fasten.*

4 Join the beaded links together by sliding the loops onto a split ring, as shown here, or by using a jump ring. Attach the pendant made in steps 1 through 2 to the split ring.

5 Fold each loose end of the leather cord over into a loop and wrap firmly with wire to secure. Trim off excess cord. Create an S-clasp in copper wire (see page 24). Add the two halves of the S-clasp to the loop ends of the leather cord.

Midnight Sky Silver Drop earrings

You can completely change the look of these earrings by using a different color or shape of bead. Keep a look out for interesting beads that you can use in different ways—you could also use unusual buttons or found objects such as shells, small pebbles, or scraps of wood with an interesting color or grain.

MATERIALS

24-gauge sterling silver wire (dead soft)

Wire cutters

Butane torch

Nylon pliers

Round-nose pliers

Pickle solution

Polishing cloth

12-gauge sterling silver wire (dead soft)

Ball-pein hammer

Bench block or anvil

Metal files

Hole punch or drill

Center punch (if using drill)

2 cube square beads or beads of choice

2 small roundel spacer beads

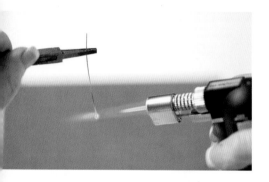

1 Create a ball at the end of a 1-in. (2.5-cm) length of 24-gauge sterling silver wire using a butane torch (see page 23). Bend the wire around into an earring wire. Repeat to make a second earring wire. Pickle, rinse, and polish to a shine.

2 Cut two pieces of 12-gauge sterling silver wire, each 1in. (2.5cm) in length. Hammer flat and texture with the ball end of the hammer. File the ends smooth and rounded. Either punch or drill a hole in each end.

3 Ball the end of a 1½-in. (4-cm) length of 24-gauge silver wire. Create a beaded dangle using a cube bead and a small spacer bead. Create a loop at the top. Attach the dangle to the hole in the flattened wire made in step 2. Repeat for the other earring.

4 Attach one of the earring wires created in step 1 to the end of one wire strip. Repeat to make up the second earring.

Dreaming in Flight Necklace

There is no reason why a necklace needs to be identical on both sides, as long as the overall design looks balanced. Lay the pieces out and rearrange them until you are happy with the look. Don't let the length of the materials list deter you from this project; simply gather all your objects together—you can add as few or as many as you want. This is the perfect necklace style to "go with your creative flow."

MATERIALS

- 0.025 (22-gauge) copper sheet
- Rubber stamp
- Pigment-based stamping inkpad
- Permanent marker
- Ferric chloride etching solution
- Jeweler's saw
- Cut Lube
- Bench block
- Files
- Liver of sulfur solution
- 400-grit sandpaper
- Drill or hole punch
- Hammer
- Dragonfly finding
- Silicone-based glue
- 2 tiny washers
- Rub 'N' Buff® Patina
- Cosmetic sponge
- 1¼in. (3cm) diameter washer
- Gear wheel
- ½in. (12mm) diameter brass washer
- Gold or brass brad
- Copper tube
- 28-gauge copper wire
- Round-nose pliers
- Bail-making pliers
- Wire cutters
- Large bead
- ¾in. (18mm) washer
- 6 round jasper beads
- 12 flat jasper beads
- 16-gauge copper wire
- Length of tarnished chain
- 2 jump rings
- 5 split rings
- 2 brass lobster clasps
- Purchased dangles

1 Stamp a design on one side of the copper sheet and color in the reverse side, using the marker pen to act as a resist. Etch as described on page 29.

2 Remove from the etching solution and cut into the desired rectangle shape. File the corners smooth and round the edges. Dip the piece in liver of sulfur and then lightly sand the surface to reveal the pattern. Drill or punch a small hole in each top corner. Glue the dragonfly on the front and small washers over the holes.

3 Add a touch of Rub 'N' Buff® patina to color the surface of the 1¼-in. (3-cm) washer. Attach the gear wheel to the washer using the glue. Attach the ½-in. (12-mm) small brass washer and the gold brad to the gear wheel with glue.

4 Cut a 3-in. (7.5-cm) length of copper tube and flatten the ends with the hammer. File the edges smooth and wrap with 28-gauge copper wire, creating a loop at each end. Bend the tube very slightly into a curve with your fingers. Wrap a 3-in. (7.5-cm) length of 28-gauge copper wire around the tubing to secure. Thread the ends through the holes in the copper rectangle and wrap to secure the rectangle to the tube.

5 Thread the end of a length of 28-gauge copper wire through the large bead and back over the bead, form a loop, and then wrap the end around the wire. Trim off any excess wire and file the ends smooth.

6 Thread the end of another piece of 28-gauge copper wire through the bead and wrap a couple of times. Next thread the end through the ¾in. (18mm) washer, and wrap around the washer twice. Wrap the remaining end around the top of the wire to secure. Trim off any excess wire and file smooth.

7 Create a beaded link using the jasper beads (see page 26), leaving a long tail of wire to wrap back around between the beads for a decorative touch. Create a double spiral random link with 16-gauge copper wire, hammered flat. Assemble the necklace with the lengths of chain, adding the clasp and dangles, and using the photos opposite and on page 73 as a guide.

Inspired by Art Necklace

When building up a design like this, you can keep adding different elements until you achieve the look you want. You can also mix and match pieces from other designs in this book, or add purchased elements. Again the letters are stamped individually, so you can say whatever you desire.

1 Cut out a ½ x 2-in. (1.5 x 2.5-cm) rectangle from the copper sheet. Glue a torn strip of paper to the front of the rectangle. Mark and drill holes for the wire and for the brass label holder. Attach the brass holder with tiny screws and nuts.

2 Hammer a series of letters of your choice into the aluminum sheet. Apply black paint to the letters. Allow to dry. Sand paint away, leaving it in the cracks.

3 Cut into separate letters and glue inside the brass holder.

MATERIALS

0.025 (22-gauge) copper sheet

Jeweler's saw

Cut Lube

Mod Podge® decoupage glue

Old page from a book or newsprint

Center punch

Drill

Small brass label holder

Tiny screws and nuts

ArtEmboss® aluminum medium
   sheet

⅛in. (2mm) alphabet metal stamps

Hammer

Bench block

Black acrylic paint

Scissors

400-grit sandpaper

Silicone-based glue

1½-in. (3.5-cm) length of ¼in. (6mm)
   copper tubing, hammered flat

1⁄16in. (1mm) WireForm® aluminum
   wire coil

Small strip of copper

Miscellaneous watch parts

24-gauge copper wire

Wire cutters

Round-nose pliers

Bail-making pliers

2-in. (5-cm) length of tarnished
   brass chain

Jump rings

18-gauge copper wire

Tweezers

Liver of sulfur solution

Leather cord

1in. (2.5cm) copper washer,
   decoupaged

4 Glue torn paper to the flattened copper tube using decoupage glue. Drill a hole in each end. Hammer a 2¼-in. (3-cm) length of aluminum wire coil flat and stick on top, then mark the hole placement and drill. Hammer a suitable word into the small strip of copper and glue it on top of the aluminum wire. Glue the watch parts to the copper strip.

5 Thread a length of 24-gauge copper wire into the holes, wrap and create a loop at each end. Attach the short length of chain to the loops. Attach the pendant to the center of the chain with a jump ring.

6 Create four wire coils with the thicker copper wire and apply liver of sulfur to tarnish. Thread the pendant onto the leather cord with two wire coils on each side. Wrap the ends of the cord with wire, leaving a loop at the top. Attach a decoupaged washer to one side, and a wire hook (see page 25) to the other.

Tips *To prevent the tarnish finish from rubbing off on the skin, after the piece is finished you can apply a light coat of paste wax and buff.*
Interesting objects can often be found at your local office supply store—such as the brass label holder used in this project; these are often used on small filing drawers.

Secrets

I like the idea of keeping a secret in full view and this little pendant is ideal to hide away a tiny thought, memento, or charm under the fabric wrapping. You could use a fragment from an old love letter for the decoupage, or hang an important keepsake from the pendant.

MATERIALS

1 x 2-in. (2.5 x 5-cm) piece of 0.032 (20-gauge) aluminum sheet
Files
Page from an old book or newsprint
Mod Podge® decoupage glue
Strips of fabric in colors of choice
Drill or ⅟₁₆in. (1.5mm) hole punch
Center punch (if using drill)
Beads in coordinating colors
24-gauge copper wire
Wire cutters
20-gauge copper wire
Leather cord
2 brass crimp beads
Jewelry pliers
Round-nose pliers
Heart charm
Jump ring

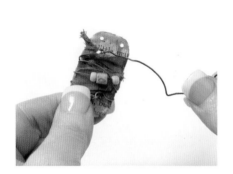

1 Round the edges of the piece of aluminum with the files and then glue paper to one side (see page 27). Wrap the piece with strips of fabric. Drill or punch two holes at the top. Thread a selection of beads onto a length of 24-gauge wire and wrap around the pendant.

2 Thread 20-gauge copper wire through one of the holes at the top of the pendant, twisting the end around the base. Trim off excess wire, leave approximately ½in. (12mm) extending. Create a coil across the top of the pendant, then thread the other end through the opposite hole and wrap to secure. Thread the pendant onto the leather cord.

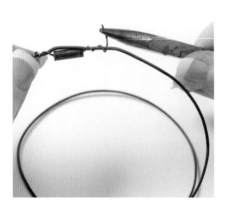

3 Thread a bead onto 24-gauge wire and wrap each end around the cord at either side of the pendant. Trim off any excess wire. Repeat for the other side.

4 Add a crimp bead at each end of the leather cord using pliers. Wrap the ends of the cord with wire, concealing the crimp beads. Create an S-hook in 24-gauge copper wire (see page 24) and attach with jump rings. Attach the hanging heart charm with a jump ring.

Poppy Ring

This is the only ring featured in the book, but the basic design is so versatile that you could make it look quite different by varying the flower shapes, and adding different colors or shapes of beads. For a simpler design, you could also just attach one large crystal or bead in the center. The finished ring resembles a poppy that dances about in the wind—the poppy center is quite loose.

MATERIALS

2-in. (5-cm) square of 26-gauge sterling silver sheet

Permanent marker

Jeweler's saw

Cut Lube

Bench pin

Files

400- and 600-grit sand paper

Texture tool with design of choice

Small regular screwdriver for texture

Circle punch

Hammer

Liver of sulfur solution

Brass brush

Polishing cloth

Hole punch or drill

20-gauge sterling silver wire (or non-tarnish silver plated wire)

Round-nose pliers

Bail-making pliers

Ring mandrel

24-gauge sterling silver wire (or non-tarnish silver-plated wire)

10–20 semi-precious coral nugget beads

10–20 head pins

1 Copy the flower template on page 125 onto the silver sheet using the permanent marker, apply cut lube to the jeweler's saw, and cut out the shape. File and refine the edges until they are smooth.

2 Use punches and other texturing tools of your choice to create the embossed design. I used a circle punch and a small screwdriver. Dip in liver of sulfur solution to highlight the punched design and then polish with the brass brush and polishing cloth. Drill a hole in the center where indicated on the template.

Tips *Make the ring slightly smaller than the necessary final size, as it will stretch slightly. Practice on inexpensive aluminum sheet metal and silver-coated wire before using sterling silver. This design also looks splendid in other metals such as copper or brass.*

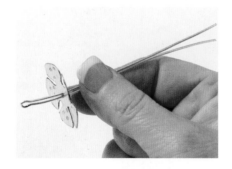

3 Fold a 12-in. (30-cm) length of 20-gauge wire in half to create a loop and thread the loop through the center hole in the flower from back to front.

4 Wrap the ends of the wire around the ring mandrel to form a ring in the size desired. Note that one wire goes clockwise and the other counterclockwise—the ends should meet at the base of the ring.

5 Wrap the base of the ring with a length of 24-gauge wire to secure the loops firmly. Snip off any excess wire and file smooth.

6 Thread the beads onto head pins, loop the end over, and cut off the excess. Attach the beaded head pins to the center loop. Shape the flower petals and refine the ring shape on the mandrel if needed.

Patina Drop Earrings

These earrings look quite complex, but they are made up of a series of simple elements. When coiling the wire, try to keep the loops quite tight to the base wire or they can begin to look rather ragged. The combination of dark colors can look a little somber, so I have added some Antique Gold Rub 'N' Buff® to brighten things up.

MATERIALS

¼in. (6mm) copper tubing
Tube cutter
Ammonia
Table salt
Plastic tub with lid or zip lock bag
20-gauge copper wire
Round-nose pliers
Bail-making pliers
24-gauge copper wire
2 faceted amethyst teardrop beads
Rub 'N' Buff® Antique Gold (optional)
Cosmetic sponge

1 Cut two pieces of tube ¾in. (2cm) long or to the desired length. Patina with the ammonia-and-salt solution as described on page 29. Remove and allow to dry. Thread 20-gauge copper wire through the tubing, creating coils and loops at each end.

2 Wrap 24-gauge wire around two lengths of the thicker wire to create the coil embellishment.

3 Add the coiled embellishments to the tubing, using the photograph opposite as a guide for positioning.

4 Coil the ends of the wire around along the front of the tubes. Make two earring wires (see page 23) and attach one to one end of each tube.

5 Create two wrapped bead dangles following the instructions on page 26. Attach to the bottom loop of the tubes. Add gold highlights to the wires using Rub 'N' Buff® if desired.

Confetti Bracelet

I became so fascinated with the way fabric and metal worked together in the Secrets necklace that I decided to use those elements as inspiration for this fun and playful bracelet. This illustrates how you can use the same basic techniques in other ways to achieve an alternative look. Never be afraid to experiment—even what seem like mistakes can turn out to be the ideal base for a totally different project.

MATERIALS

1 x 6in. (2.5 x 15cm) piece of 0.032 (20-gauge) aluminum sheet

Scissors

Files

Page from an old book or newsprint

Mod Podge® decoupage glue

Strips of patterned fabric in color of choice

1⁄16in. (2mm) hole punch

12 Tim Holtz Ideology trinket pins

6 x 3mm round beads

12 small square beads

24-gauge copper wire with patina and tarnish

Round-nose pliers

Bail-making pliers

20-gauge galvanized steel wire

Wire cutters

Length of tarnished brass chain

9 x ⅜in. (1cm) brass nuts

6 faceted iridescent glass beads

6 head pins

6 gunmetal swivel pins

17 jump rings

Lobster clasp

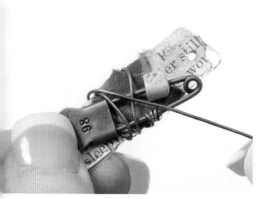

1 Cut twelve ½ x 1-in. (1.2 x 2.5-cm) asymmetrical rectangle shapes from the aluminum. Round the corners with scissors and file smooth. Decoupage scraps of the book pages onto both sides and then wrap in strips of fabric. Punch a hole at one end. Thread one or two beads onto each trinket pin and wrap with copper wire to secure to the rectangle.

2 Working off the spool, thread the end of the steel wire through the hole in the top of one of the rectangles and wrap to secure. Cut off the spool, leaving a 2-in. (5-cm) end. Create a half-loop, thread the half loop onto the chain, and close. Wrap the end of the wire to secure, and then trim off any excess. Repeat for the other 11 rectangles, spacing them along the chain.

3 Wrap a length of steel wire around the brass nut to make a dangle. Make another eight dangles the same. Attach to the chain with jump rings, spaced equally along the length.

Tip *Visit the fishing department of a sporting goods store to look for interesting elements such as swivels and spinners. It's a great way to add a fun feeling to your designs.*

4 Create six dangles with the remaining beads and headpins as described on page 26. Attach the bead dangles to swivel pins and then to the chain with jump rings.

5 Tie on strips of fabric at random and then trim as necessary. Add the lobster clasp with jump rings.

Tattered and Torn Necklace

Using fabric strips adds a whole new element to your designs. You don't need any sewing skills—these are simply strips ripped from lengths of dyed muslin fabric. The frayed edges of the fabric not only soften the effect of all the metal, but also create an interesting contrast with the regimented repetition of the chain links.

MATERIALS

⅞in. (2.25cm) washer
Page from an old book
Mod Podge® decoupage glue
Distressing ink
Cosmetic sponge
Two-part resin
Toothpick
Scissors
20-gauge copper wire
Wire cutters
½in. (12mm) copper pipe
Pipe cutter
Bail-making pliers
Round-nose pliers
Permanent marker
Ferric chloride etching solution
Liver of sulfur solution
Brass brush
16-in. (40-cm) strips of several different fabrics
2 lengths of link chain
2 large oval links
16 turquoise nugget beads
24-gauge copper wire
Leather cord
Crimp beads

1 Decoupage a scrap of the paper onto the washer (see page 27). Sponge some ink onto the paper to distress it a little.

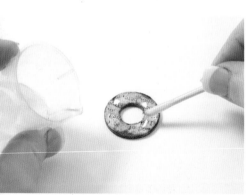

2 Mix the resin following the instructions on page 28. Apply a little resin over the washer using the toothpick and set aside to dry overnight. When dry, trim off any excess resin with scissors and wrap the washer with 20-gauge wire, using the photograph opposite as a guide.

Tips *It helps to arrange the objects if the necklace is hanging up. Pin it to a piece of thick foam board as you are working, so you can see how the dangles and objects hang.*
This project has just one washer for the focal, but you can string on as many objects of your choice as desired.
Repeat the same basic instructions to create a matching bracelet.
Alternatively, create memory charms such as those used in the Circle the Globe Bracelet on page 106, or add keys, purchased charms, or even textured ribbon.

3 Cut a ¾-in. (2-cm) length of copper pipe. Using a black permanent marker, draw a design to be etched on the surface. Etch as described on page 29.

6 Create a beaded link with three of the turquoise nugget beads and 24-gauge copper wire and attach to the chain as shown above. Repeat on the other side. Create a dangle with two nuggets and hang from the center of the chain. Add the washer to the base of the dangle.

4 Clean the etching solution and the resist from the tube. Dip in liver of sulfur and then brush up some areas with the brass brush to highlight elements of the design. Thread several strips of torn fabric through the tube.

5 Add one large oval link to one end of one chain. Thread one set of fabric strip ends through the link and fold over, then wrap with 20-gauge wire to secure. Trim off excess fabric. Repeat with the other oval link at the other end of the chain.

7 Create two beaded links with the eight remaining nuggets and add one to each oval link. Cut an 8-in. (20-cm) length of cord, thread through the end of one beaded link, and fold it in half, matching the ends. Wrap with 24-gauge copper wire at the base, near the oval link. Repeat on the other side. Pinch crimp beads onto the end of each doubled cord with pliers and add an S-hook fastener (see page 24).

Trinkets

Making your own jewelry offers an ideal opportunity to incorporate found objects and designs that mean something to you, or which will have a meaning for the recipient. On this necklace the charms could recall important events, or the decoupage could feature some kind of relevant text.

1 Cut a circle of printed paper to fit into each bottle cap and stamp each with a butterfly design. Place the paper disks in the caps and fill with resin, adding glitter if desired. Put the three caps aside to set overnight. Decoupage a scrap of printed paper onto each washer (see page 27). Sponge some ink onto the paper to distress a little. Apply a little resin over each washer with the toothpick and set aside to dry overnight.

2 Turn the three bottle caps over and glue a soda can tab on either side of each cap in line, using the silicone-based glue.

3 Thread the wide ribbon in and out through the tabs on the three bottle caps. Begin threading from front to back, then back to front, continuing in this way.

MATERIALS

3 bottle caps

Printed paper designs

Circle punch to match size of bottle cap

Butterfly stamp

Brown stamping pigment-based inkpad

Two-part resin

Gold glitter (optional)

3 x ¾in. (15mm) steel washers, pickled and aged

Mod Podge® decoupage glue

Toothpick

6 soda can tabs

Silicone-based glue

1yd (90cm) of ½in. (12mm) wide tattered green fabric ribbon

1yd (90cm) of ¼in. (5mm) wide tattered green fabric ribbon

Scissors

12in. (30cm) of 20-gauge copper wire

Round-nose pliers

Miscellaneous charms

Jump rings

2½in. (6.5cm) tarnished brass chain

2 beads

2 head pins

2 gold spacer beads

2 jasper 2mm round beads

2 x 1-in. (2.5-cm) lengths of tarnished brass chain

4 Cut the narrow ribbon in half lengthwise and thread the loop through the end tab.

5 Thread the loose ends of this same ribbon through the loop just made and pull to secure. Repeat for the other side.

6 Knot all three strands of fabric together near the tab. Create another knot at the other end. Trim the ends if necessary and then repeat steps 4 through 6 on the other side.

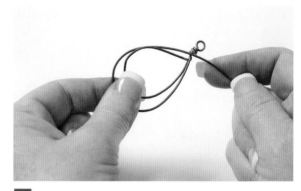

7 Working off the spool of 20-gauge copper wire, create a wire loop and wrap the end around the loop to secure. Begin forming the teardrop/circle shape. Wrap the wire around several times.

8 Cut off the wire from the spool, leaving a 2-in (5-cm) end. Wrap the wire around decoratively to secure in place.

9 Attach several assorted charms to one of the strands at the base of the wire teardrop, using jump rings.

10 Attach one of the decoupaged washers to the ring at the top of the wire teardrop, using another jump ring.

11 Attach the wire teardrop to the center of the 2½-in. (6.5-cm) length of tarnished brass chain, using a jump ring. Attach the ends of the chain to the tabs on either side of the central bottle cap.

12 Create two beaded dangles (see page 26) on head pins using beads and spacer beads. Attach to necklace, using the photo as a placement guide.

13 Thread a 1-in. (2.5-cm) chain through one of the remaining washers. Take the end of the chain through the inner tab on one of the side bottle caps, bring it round, and attach it to the final link at the other end of the chain. Repeat on the other side.

Steampunk Wire Bracelet

Although this is possibly the most complex project in this chapter, it is assembled from smaller elements that all use simple techniques such as wire wrapping and bending. The design is freeform so you can do just whatever you like to achieve a similar look—no two bracelets will be exactly the same and really you cannot make a mistake.

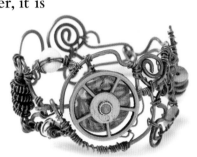

1 Anneal all the copper rods in the flame of the torch (see page 33). Cut off a length around 2in. (5cm) long and thread it through the disk bead. Make a loop at each end. Take another length of rod, make a loop at the end and hook around the wire bar at the top. Take it around the outside of the disk bead and hook the bar at the bottom. Cut off any excess rod. Repeat on the other side of the disk bead. Make few zigzags with pliers and add as a decorative element.

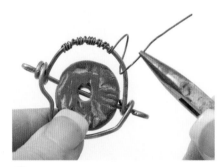

2 Wrap 24-gauge copper wire around the outer curved rod on one side of the disk bead to embellish.

MATERIALS

4 x 12-in. (30-cm) WireForm® thin copper rods

Butane torch

Pickle solution

Wire cutters

1in. (2.5cm) disk bead

Round-nose pliers

24-gauge copper wire

9 x 3mm assorted disk beads

1in. (2.5cm) gear wheel

⅜in. (1cm) brass washer

Brass watch winder

Silicone-based glue

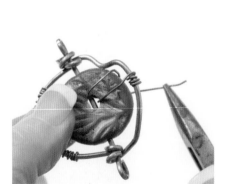

3 Wrap 24-gauge copper wire around the other side of the outer curved rod and through the center of the disk bead. This holds the disk bead in place and stops it from spinning.

4 Fold one of the 12-in. (30-cm) rods in half. Create a loop at the top, similar to the one shown in the picture, then create random curves along the length of each side, finishing in spirals. Repeat to create a second curved length, with the end spirals pointing away from each other.

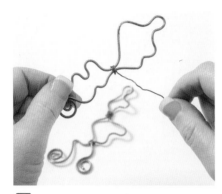

5 Wrap 24-gauge copper wire around the rods at intervals along the design, wherever the curves of each side come toward one another. Make the other side of the bracelet in the same way.

6 Cut a 2-in. (5-cm) length of 24-gauge copper wire and wrap it loosely with another length of the same wire.

7 Cut a 2-in. (5-cm) length of copper rod and make a loop at each end. Wrap it with the coiled wire made in step 6. Wrap the ends of the wire around the rod to secure.

8 Open one loop on the focal piece made in steps 1 through 3 and attach it to one of the sides. Repeat on the other side.

9 Using the 24-gauge wire, begin adding wire embellishments between the central focal piece and the side, adding beads at random as you work.

10 Continue adding more wiring between and around the rods of the side pieces, still threading on different beads as you work. Repeat on the other side of the bracelet.

11 Stack the gear wheel, washer, and watch winder and glue together. Attach to the front of the main focal with glue. Form the bracelet into a loop to fit around your wrist.

12 Create a fastening loop at one end of the bracelet and bend the other end into a matching hook.

Tip *If additional length is needed, simply add another link at the base of the bracelet.*

CHAPTER 4
Metalwork

In this chapter we move on to some projects that require soldering and other metalcrafting skills. Don't be afraid—all of these are very simple to learn if you follow the instructions carefully! Being able to attach metal permanently together will make your jewelry more durable and you can create effects that will rival those of professional jewelry-makers.

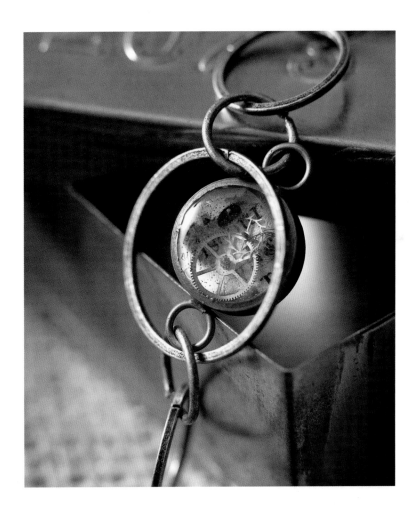

Autumn Leaves Earrings

The first project in this chapter is a really simple one to introduce you to soldering, which is a skill that will allow you to develop your jewelry in a great many ways. I've chosen these pretty vine leaf findings, but there is an almost limitless choice of shapes and styles in pre-made findings to choose from.

MATERIALS

16-gauge copper wire
Wire cutters
Hammer
Bench block
Pickle solution
Flux
2 leaf findings
Solder
Butane torch or soldering iron
Firebrick
Brass brush
Round-nose pliers
Bail-making pliers
400-grit sandpaper
Liver of sulfur solution
Tweezers or tongs
24-gauge copper wire
2 small green beads

1 Cut two 2-in. (5-cm) lengths of 16-gauge wire and flatten one end of each length with the hammer. Clean in pickle solution.

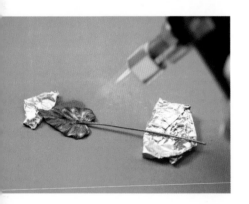

2 Apply flux to the top of each leaf where the wire will be placed. Lay the flattened end of the wire on the top of the leaf and place a small solder chip on each side of the wire. Heat with the torch until the solder melts and flows into the join. Repeat with other leaf. Dip both pieces in pickle and finish with the brass brush.

Tip *When soldering, you can fold pieces of aluminum foil to use as props to hold the pieces at the proper level or correct angle.*

3 Use the pliers to curve each wire around into an ear wire shape. Sand the ends smooth. Dip the earrings into liver of sulfur to add patina.

4 Create two beaded dangles with the 24-gauge wire and the green beads, as described on page 26. Thread one beaded dangle onto each earring wire to hang in front of the leaf and hide the soldered joins.

Dancing Dreams Necklace

This project covers a slightly different soldering technique, this time using a soldering iron instead of the butane torch. The soldering iron does not get as hot as the flame of a torch. This design has lots of excitement and movement to catch the eye and was inspired by Susan Lenart–Kazmir, an artist whose work I've long admired.

MATERIALS

2 images of your choice
2 glass 1-in. (2.5-cm) square tiles
Copper tape
Round-nose pliers
Bail-making pliers
Flux
Solder
Solder iron
Firebrick
Third hand
2 copper jump rings
6 ball head pins
24-gauge copper wire
Purchased dangle
2 lengths of narrow ribbon
2 box style cord ends
Clasp of choice
3 jump rings
Short length of chain

1 Sandwich two images back to back between two square glass tiles. Wrap copper tape around the outside edge of the two tiles.

2 Using the back of one of the metal tools, burnish the edges of the tape over the edges of the glass to hold everything in place.

3 Brush the copper tape with flux. Add a ball of solder to the tip of the soldering iron. Slide the tip of the iron along the tape to paint on the solder. Repeat around all four sides.

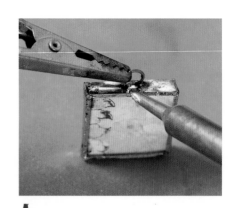

4 Using the third hand to hold the jump ring in place, solder the ring at the top of the pendant. Add another jump ring at the bottom.

5 Bunch the head pins together roughly and wrap randomly with the copper wire. Add to the top of the pendant and add the purchased dangle at the bottom. Thread the pendant onto the ribbon.

6 Knot the ribbons together at each end. Place a cord end over the knot and press each side flat with pliers. Repeat on the other side. Trim off any excess ribbon ends. Attach the clasp and chain to the loops on the cord ends with jump rings.

Art Deco Spiral Earrings

A simple and elegant pair of earrings, which feature an attractive art deco-style design. The contrast between the two different metals is a vital feature of this design—most metals can be soldered together quite easily.

1 With a jeweler's saw cut two matching pendant shapes from copper sheet using the template on page 125. Drill a hole in the top end of each. File all the edges smooth. Cut a short length of brass rod and coil one end with the round-nose pliers.

2 Hammer the coil flat. Pickle the metal. Apply flux and then solder the brass coil to the earring pendant, as described on page 32. Pickle again and then brush with the brass brush.

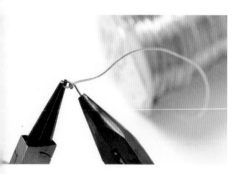

3 Working off the spool of 24-gauge copper wire, create a loop and wrap the end of the wire around the base of the loop.

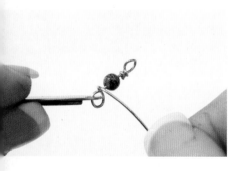

4 Thread on a bead and finish with a loop and wire. Attach to the earring pendants with jump rings and add earring wires.

MATERIALS

0.025 (22-gauge) copper sheet
Jeweler's saw
Cut Lube
Drill or punch
Files
16-gauge brass rod
Round-nose pliers
Bail-making pliers
Ball-pein hammer
Bench block
Pickle solution
Flux
Solder
Butane torch
Firebrick
Brass brush
24-gauge copper wire
2 x 2mm green jasper beads
2 jump rings
Pair of earring wires

Tip *Remember to solder the spirals so that they coil in opposite directions to create a pair of earrings. You could make a larger pendant and use it as the focal piece for a matching necklace.*

Circle the Globe Bracelet

The circular charms in this bracelet contain a selection of tiny found items, so when making it you can select pieces that hold memories for the wearer. This project introduces casting with resin, which you can mix and pour yourself—it is ideal to hold such small pieces safe and protected within a design.

MATERIALS

Length of ½in. (12mm) copper tubing

Tube cutter

Files

24-gauge copper wire

Wire cutters

Round-nose pliers

Bail-making pliers

Pickle solution

Piece of metal foil

Flux

Solder

Butane torch

Firebrick

Liver of sulfur solution

Sticky or packing tape

Two-part resin

Page from old book

Letters or number embellishments

Selection of watch parts

Scissors or sharp knife

Purchased large tarnished silver links

Jump rings

18-gauge sterling silver wire

Hammer

Bench block

1 Cut the copper tubing into three ¼-in. (5-mm) sections using the tube cutter. File the ends smooth and remove any burrs. Create jump rings from copper wire, as described on page 22.

2 Pickle all the pieces. Solder a jump ring to each side of the tube rings as described on page 32. Allow to cool completely before moving, to give the joints time to set so that they will not come apart. Pickle and clean all the pieces. Dip in liver of sulfur solution if a tarnished effect is desired.

3 Press all the rings of copper tube ring firmly onto a length of packing tape to create a backing for the resin when casting.

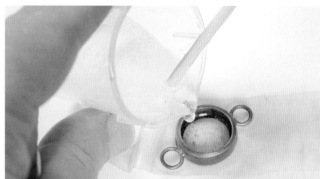

4 Mix the resin according to the manufacturer's instructions and pour a little into each copper tube ring.

5 Add a scrap of printed paper from the old book page and a selection of other embellishments on top of the resin layer, to create different charms.

6 Fill the charm mold to the top with resin. Set aside and allow the resin to cure for at least 24 hours.

7 When the resin is completely hard, carefully peel off the packing tape from the back of the charms.

10 Create a hook from 18-gauge silver wire (see page 25). Texture and dip in liver of sulfur solution. Attach the hook to the ends of the bracelet with jump rings or by using one of the links on the chain.

8 If any resin has leaked out, clean up with scissors or a sharp knife. You can add additional resin if necessary to fill up the charm, then allow further time to cure.

Tips *Do not move the copper tube ring after adding the jump ring until the solder has hardened and cooled. After pouring the resin, remove any undesired air bubbles by gently blowing on the surface through a straw. Links can be taken from a purchased chain for this project. If they are soldered together, use wire cutters to open them, attach the charm and then resolder using a soldering iron.*

9 Use large copper jump rings to attach each charm inside one of the silver rings, and to join each ring to the next to create the bracelet.

Copper Bangle

The ideal design for the man in your life, this heavy copper bangle features wrapped wire, a washer, and imitation rivets so it couldn't be more masculine. However, the simple design is also very stylish and effective and will be sure to catch the eye of the most sophisticated man–about–town.

1 Hammer both ends of the copper tubing flat and then round off the ends neatly with a file.

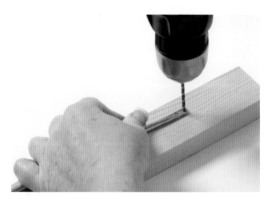

2 Drill two holes in line with each other through one of the flattened ends. Repeat at the other end of the tubing.

3 Insert a very tiny screw into each of the four drilled holes in the tubing.

MATERIALS

8in. (20cm) of ¼in. (5mm) copper tubing

Hammer

Bench block

Files

Center punch

Drill

Four small screws

Cutting disk for mini-drill or industrial wire cutters

Bracelet mandrel (optional)

¾in. (7.5mm) copper washer

Butane torch

Pickle solution

⅟₁₆in. (1mm) WireForm® aluminum wire

Solder

Flux

Firebrick

Round-nose pliers

Bail-making pliers

Liver of sulfur solution

4 Cut off any excess length of screw on the reverse side, so that the ends are flush with the surface. Use eye protection when using the cutting disk.

7 Shape the tubing into a bracelet with your hands, bringing the ends together and overlapping them by the diameter of the washer. Use the bracelet mandrel to achieve the size if necessary.

5 Hammer the end of each screw on the reverse side to flatten it slightly and prevent it from falling out.

8 Anneal the washer with the butane torch (see page 33).

6 File off any burrs so that the reverse of the bracelet is smooth.

9 Drop the washer into the pickle solution (see page 33). Remove and hammer the surface to texture it. Drill a series of holes around the washer. Place a short length of aluminum wire in each hole and hammer flat to create the look of rivets.

10 Set the washer between the two ends of the bracelet. Apply flux to the areas and add solder chips. Heat with the torch to solder, as described on page 32. Pickle the bracelet to clean it up again.

11 Wrap a length of aluminum wire around the back section of the bracelet for extra embellishment. Reshape the around the mandrel, if necessary. Apply some liver of sulfur to highlight the textured areas.

Tip *The sizes given will create a bracelet to fit a standard 7-in. (17.5-cm) wrist—use a longer piece of tubing for a larger wrist, or a shorter piece for a smaller one.*

Autumn Fire Earrings

You can make these earrings to go with specific outfits by using different color beads. The large silver links are soldered, which means there is no danger that they will pull apart when the earrings are worn. Sterling silver wire can be the best option for the earring wires—you can use premade ones if you prefer.

MATERIALS

16-gauge sterling silver wire
Wire cutters
Round-nose pliers
Bail-making pliers
Files
Paste flux
Easy silver solder
Butane torch
Pickle solution
Bench block
Hammer
Polishing cloth
28-gauge sterling silver sheet
Disk cutter
Pencil
Hole punch or drill
Center punch (if using drill)
Dapping block and punches
2 silver head pins
2 flat spacer beads
2 round 2mm spacer beads
2 cube-shaped dyed beads
Pair of earring wires

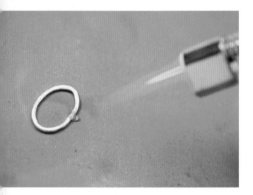

1 Create a loop in 16-gauge sterling silver wire, file the ends flat, and push them together. Set the ring onto a firebrick and apply paste flux. Add an easy solder chip and solder the ring closed. Pickle the loop, then hammer flat. Add texture to the surface if desired, then polish to the desired shine. Repeat to make a second loop.

2 To make the bead cap, cut a ½in. (12mm) circle from the silver sheet. Mark the hole in the base with a pencil and punch or drill. If drilling the hole, use a center punch before drilling.

3 Use the dapping block and a matching punch to shape the piece into a dome-shaped bead cap.

4 Thread a spacer bead, large bead and the bead cap onto each head pin. Create a loop in the end of the head pin to finish. Trim off any excess wire. Attach the loop of each dangle to the silver loops made in step 1 and attach one to each earring wire.

Saturn Earrings

The name of this project was inspired by the planet Saturn, with its encircling rings. I have created a textured and tarnished finish for the metal in this design, but it would also look very effective with the metal all buffed to a high shine, as in the Tricolor Droplet Earrings on page 50.

(Tricolor Droplet Earrings on page 50)

MATERIALS

- 26-gauge sterling silver sheet
- Disk cutter
- Files
- Hole punch or drill
- Bench block
- Ball-pein hammer
- Texturing hammer
- Dapping block and punches
- 24-gauge copper wire
- 24-gauge silver wire
- Round-nose pliers
- Bail-making pliers
- Flux
- Solder
- Butane torch
- Firebrick or ceramic tile
- 4 jump rings
- Liver of sulfur solution
- Brass brush
- Pair of earring wires

1 Cut two disks from the silver sheet. File all the edges reasonably smooth and use the punch to make a small hole at the top of each disk.

2 Create texture across the surface of each disk, using the grooved side of the texturing hammer.

3 Place each disk in turn in the largest recess in the dapping block and tap with the matching punch to shape into a shallow dome.

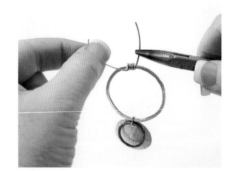

4 Make two large rings in copper wire (see page 22) and two larger ones in silver wire. Hammer both to flatten and texture—you can also solder the ends. For each earring, join one copper ring, one disk, and one silver ring together using a jump ring. Wrap the base of the silver ring with a short length of copper wire.

5 Dip the earrings in liver of sulfur solution to add patina. Rinse off and dry. Polish the copper disk and wire wrapping only with the brass brush to add some contrast. Add the earring wires.

Forget-Me-Not

This charming flower necklace is deceptively simple—don't attempt it until you have practiced soldering a few times, since it needs to be soldered in several stages. Apart from this, the design uses standard techniques covered in previous projects. When you have some metalworking confidence, you can choose to add more leaves or additional stems.

MATERIALS

- 26-gauge sterling silver sheet
- Jeweler's saw
- Cut Lube
- Bench pin
- Files
- 400-grit sandpaper
- Texture tools of choice
- Hand punch
- Hammer
- Bench block
- 18-gauge sterling silver wire
- Butane torch
- Paste flux
- Hard solder
- Firebrick
- Wire cutters
- Medium solder
- Easy solder
- Round-nose pliers
- Bail-making pliers
- Purchased silver chain
- Liver of sulfur solution
- Polishing cloth

1 Using the template on page 125, cut out the flower and a leaf from the silver sheet, using a saw. File the edges smooth and refine the shape if necessary. Add the texture lines to the petals. Punch a hole in the center of the flower.

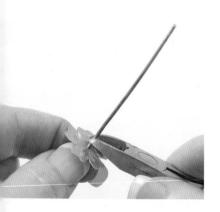

2 Make a ball in the end of the 18-gauge wire with the torch, as described on page 23. Insert the wire into the hole, with the ball in the center of the flower. Flux and solder, using a hard solder chip, on the back of the flower. The solder should flow through the crack and hold the wire in place. Trim the excess wire flush and sand smooth.

3 Cut a length of silver wire for the stem and hammer flat. Add a texture to both the stem and the leaf. Flux the leaf area and add medium solder chips. Solder the leaf to the stem and then attach the stem to the flower in the same way, using easy solder chips.

4 Place the flower face side down on the firebrick and solder a short length of silver wire at the top of the pendant. Bend the wire around to create a loop. Hang the flower on the silver chain.

5 Dip the entire necklace in liver of sulfur solution to add patina. Polish some areas of patina away.

All Geared Up

This is one of those projects where you can use up all those bits and pieces left over from other projects. Each of the five sections has different embellishments and it really does not matter what you use, as long as it fits in with the overall look. You could also stamp words onto strips of metal and attach with nuts and bolts or rivets.

MATERIALS

0.025 (22-gauge) copper sheet
  copper sheet
0.032 (20-gauge) brass sheet
Jeweler's saw
Cut Lube
Bench pin
Files
400-grit sandpaper
Hammer
Bench block
Center punch
Drill
Tarnished metal eyelets
Miscellaneous gears and watch parts
Small brass/copper/aluminum or
  steel washers
1/16in. (1mm) x 0.014 copper tubing
1in. (2.5cm) square wire mesh
Tiny nuts, bolts, and screws
Small screwdriver
20-gauge silver wire
16-gauge copper wire
Round-nose pliers
Bail-making pliers
Awl or needle
3/8in. (8mm) jump ring maker or
  dowel rod
Liver of sulfur
Tweezers
Brass brush

1 Using the templates on page 124, cut out three shapes from the copper sheet and two from the brass sheet, using a jeweler's saw. File the edges smooth with a metal file and finish with 400-grit sandpaper. Add texture to each piece with the hammer.

2 Arrange the pieces alternately: copper, brass, copper, brass, copper. Mark the position of eyelet holes with the center punch and drill the holes. Set the eyelets as described on page 31.

3 Arrange the gears and other embellishments on the pieces and move them around until you are happy with the design. Mark the placement of holes, and then center punch and drill as necessary to attach the embellishments.

4 Attach some of the embellishments to each of the sections using the tiny nuts, bolts, and screws.

5 Attach some of the pieces by "stitching" them on with lengths of wire. Coil lengths of wire, hammer them flat, and attach them to the bracelet by lacing with wire. Create a loop on the end of one piece using copper wire.

6 Make eight large jump rings using the copper wire and use them to join the five sections together. Create a fastening hook on the end of the bracelet (see page 25) to match the end loop.

7 Dip the bracelet briefly in liver of sulfur solution until tarnished. Dry and finish with the brass brush to highlight some areas of the design.

Templates

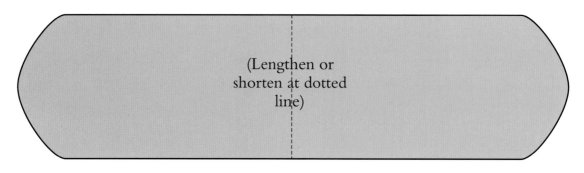

(Lengthen or shorten at dotted line)

Material Girl (see page 58)

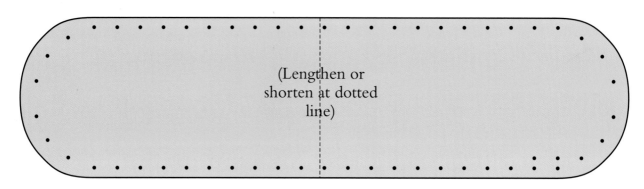

(Lengthen or shorten at dotted line)

Copper Cuff (see page 42)

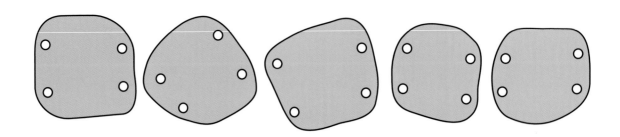

All Geared Up (see page 120)

Hanging My Heart
Necklace (see page 48)

Poppy Ring
(see page 80)

Forget-Me-Not Necklace
(see page 118)

Old World Earrings (see page 40)
Art Deco Earrings (see page 104)

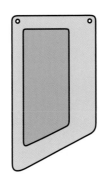

Sunray Pendant
(see page 56)

Windsurf Earrings
(see page 64)

Time Warp Necklace
(see page 52) (Base)

Time Warp Necklace
(Inset)

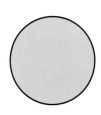

Circle

RESOURCES

Linda Peterson Designs
www.lindapetersondesigns.com

US SUPPLIERS

General craft materials and tools.

A.C. Moore
1-888-226-6673
www.acmoore.com

Hobby Lobby Stores
www.hobbylobby.com

JoAnn Crafts
1-888-739-4120
www.joann.com

Michaels Stores
1800-642-4235
www.michaels.com

ONLINE RETAILERS

*Metalsmith supplies,
tools, beads, and metal stamps.*

Artbeads.com
www.artbeads.com

Beaducation
www.beaducation.com

Rings N Things
www.rings-things.com

Rio Grande
www.riogrande.com

*Sheet metal—copper, brass, and
aluminum*

K& S Engineering
www.ksmetals.com

HARDWARE SUPPLIERS

*Specialty nuts, bolts, and copper
sheeting and pipe*

Ace Hardware
www.acehardware.com

Home Depot
www.homedepot.com

Lowe's Inc.
www.lowes.com

OTHER MATERIALS

Alcohol inks

Ranger Inc.
www.rangerink.com

Alphabet charms

Making Memories
Vintage Groove by Jill Schwartz
www.makingmemories.com/
jillschwartz

Beadalon, Inc.
www.beadalon.com

Envirotex Light two-part resin

ETI
www.eti-usa.com

Mod Podge®

Plaid Enterprises
www.plaidonline.com

*Rub-N-Buff®, ArtEmboss®,
WireForm® and Friendly Plastic®*

Amaco., Inc.
www.amaco.com

UK SUPPLIERS

Cookson Precious Metals
0121 200 2120
www.CooksonGold.com

Hobbycraft
0845 051 6599
www.hobbycraft.co.uk

International Craft
01923 235 336
www.internationalcraft.com

John Lewis
Tel: 08456 049 049
www.johnlewis.com

The Scientific Wire Co.
020 8505 0002
www.wires.co.uk

Wirejewellery.co.uk
www.wirejewellery.co.uk

Index

Acknowledgments

Just as they say it takes a town to raise a child, it takes a great team to create a book! While I may be the name on the front cover, this book is not possible without the help of my great team—my publisher, Cindy Richards and her talented team, Sally, Dawn and Liz; my personal editor, Marie Clayton, who spent endless hours pouring over my words; my photographer, Geoff Dann, who is brilliant at making my work shine, and his assistant, Marc Harvey. Thanks also to Stuart West and Luis Peral-Aranda for the style photography. Thank you all for each of your talents and efforts into creating this book! You are the best!

I also have to thank my family: my husband, Dana, and kids for jumping in and getting things done while I poured my soul into this book. This is a sacrifice of love from you to me. I love you all!